Record Breakers of the North Atlantic

Record Breakers
of the North Atlantic

Blue Riband Liners 1838-1952

Arnold Kludas

Including thirty-five drawings of all the Blue Riband ships
by Dietmar Borchert

CHATHAM PUBLISHING

LONDON

Frontispiece: The Hapag *Deutschland*, in a painting by Hans Bohrdt

Copyright © Koehlers Verlagsgesellschaft 1999

First published in Great Britain in 2000 by
Chatham Publishing,
61 Frith Street,
London W1V 5TA

Chatham Publishing is an imprint of Gerald Duckworth & Co Ltd

Translated from *Das Blaue Band des Nordatlantiks*, first published
in Germany by Koehlers Verlagsgesellschaft mbH in 1999

British Library Cataloguing in Publication Data
A catalogue record for this book is available from the British Library

ISBN 1 86176 141 4

Translated by Keith Thomas

Typeset by Tony Hart, Isle of Wight
Printed and bound in China by Midas Printing Ltd

Contents

In this impressive and informative poster from the 1950s Cunard White Star offered all the superlatives: the *Queen Mary* as the world's fastest ship, and the *Queen Elizabeth* as the world's largest.

Europe to all America

R.M.S QUEEN ELIZABETH
LEAVING THE OCEAN
TERMINAL SOUTHAMPTON

Foreword

THIS BOOK represents the history of the contest between international passenger liner companies for the fastest crossing of the North Atlantic. The competition never existed officially, and in the early stages the expression Blue Riband was not even used; nevertheless, the contest certainly took place, and for many decades the term 'fight for the Blue Riband' was a familiar one – and with every justification. In the maritime world only *one* other subject has acquired equally legendary status, and that is the myth of the *Titanic*. These two subjects certainly have one thing in common: until very recent times much of the written matter about the Blue Riband and the *Titanic* has been mainly nonsensical.

From the earliest days when I began writing about international passenger liners – some thirty years ago – I was always aware of the many contradictions to be found in the written material about the Blue Riband. I found it particularly annoying that in nearly all the sources there was no differentiation between record passages made in the different directions – westbound and eastbound voyages. This often meant that two different vessels were claimed to be the holders of the Blue Riband simultaneously. In many of my publications I have attempted to make well researched contributions to the debate, and in this book I have tried to interpret the sources concerning the Blue Riband in such a way as to arrive at correct and historically well-founded conclusions.

My heartfelt thanks to all those kind people who have actively assisted me in this project. At the outset I wish to give a posthumous mention to two gentle-men who followed the same path as myself for many long years, albeit in past decades: Noel R P Bonsor, whose book *North Atlantic Seaway* has been virtually my 'Bible' for more than forty-five years; and John H Isherwood, whose column 'Steamers of the Past' in the monthly *Sea Breezes* has been obligatory reading for any lover of maritime and technological history since 1949.

I also wish to express my gratitude to two close friends for the drawings of all the Blue Riband ships published in this book, together with the emblems of the shipping companies which took part in the contest. Dietmar Borchert has drawn each of the thirty-six ships in his inimitable style, most of them in colour. J F Horst Koenig produced the full-colour shipping company emblems, which are shown here for the first time as a complete and correct collection. To both men I offer my heartfelt thanks, not only for their impressive artistic endeavours, but also for the intensive research work they had to carry out in order to produce such accurate artwork.

Eckhard Biermann, Harro Christiansen and Clas Broder Hansen, as well as the Deutsches Schiffartsmuseum and Julian Mannering from Chatham Publishing provided valuable support for my project.

Very special and heartfelt thanks also to my wife, Ilse, without whose patience, help and understanding this book would not have been possible.

ARNOLD KLUDAS

Kaiser Wilhelm der Grosse ushered in the era of the super-liner.

The Rules of the Blue Riband

BEFORE the advent of aircraft, ships represented the sole method of overseas transport. This fact alone explains the constant striving for ever larger and faster ships, which was simply a logical response to economic necessity. In this respect the battle for the Blue Riband – the unofficial trophy for the fastest sea crossing of the North Atlantic – was a reflection of continuing technological development. But, especially after 1930,

national pride, defence issues and politics were also powerful influences and taxpayers' money was used liberally in the development and building of these record-breaking passenger liners.

But what was the Blue Riband? Why does it still fascinate us? And what were the rules which regulated the competition for this prize for which the shipping companies so keenly fought? And if there were indeed rules, why were there so many confus-

A splendid reception for the *Normandie* on 3 June 1935, entering New York as the latest winner of the Blue Riband.

Cunard
Line luggage tag
showing the *Queen Mary*.

ing contradictions, which caused many an interested observer to despair? Many authors have already come to grief in attempting to answer these questions, just as several generations of experts have disputed the pros and cons of the different arguments. In fact, the whole notion is really quite simple, and a little logical thought soon produces an explanation.

First, we have to understand that the Blue Riband has never been an official distinction, and was never endowed or granted by any institution or authority. The Blue Riband did not even have a physical manifestation, such as a blue pennant, although now and then a ship's captain did have a Blue Riband made and hoisted. It is also true that the competition never had official rules of play laid down. The Hales Trophy, donated in 1935, was never its official trophy, as will be explained later.

UNWRITTEN RULES

The 'rules' which did exist and which were closely observed, thanks largely to the journalists of the time, were unwritten ones. The record voyages were a popular subject in the newspapers, and particularly in New York, the primary destination of the Atlantic crossings, and the knowledgeable reporters in that great international metropolis virtually acted as referees, watching over the shipping companies and their captains to ensure that they adhered to the unwritten rules fairly and correctly. These conditions were never laid down, but developed gradually over many years, and were silently acknowledged by the participants. The term Blue Riband was borrowed from the world of horse racing, and it was around 1890 when journalists first applied it to record voyages across the North Atlantic, although it did not come into general use until the start of the twentieth century. Until then the subject of discussion was simply 'record voyages'. In fact, record crossings had existed from as early as 1838, when the *Sirius*, the first passenger ship to enter regular North Atlantic service, was trumped by the *Great Western*; the latter's speed of 8.66 knots surpassing that of the *Sirius* at 8.03 knots.

What were the conditions which a passenger ship had to fulfil in order to win the distinction of the Blue Riband? First, she had

to cross the Atlantic at a higher average speed than the current holder of the Blue Riband. Second, the record crossing had to take place in the westbound direction, i.e. from Europe to America.

It has already been mentioned that the Blue Riband has been the subject of much written material including many contradictory documents; in fact, most of the published material fails to take into account these two conditions and to understand the reasons for this we need to consider a number of factors.

Rapidity can be expressed either in terms of time or of speed. The time, or in this case the duration of the crossing between two locations, may vary according to the course steered, i.e. it does not necessarily tell us which ship is faster than another. The average speed, on the other hand, can be calculated to within a fraction of a knot, and that is the reason why the ships' actual average speed for the crossing was adopted as the standard criterion, rather than the duration of the journey.

In many ways it seems more logical to compare crossing times; after all, what is the point of a passenger travelling on a faster ship if it arrives at its destination later than the slower vessel? With this in mind it is important to understand that the calculated speeds stated in all the record tables relating to the Blue Riband only include the open seas part of the voyage, i.e. that part of the crossing in which the ship can steam at full speed. (See the table on page 146.) Naturally, different starting points result in different distances from the destination, so any ship taking a shorter route would therefore be favoured by a simple time measurement. So the only way to ensure fair and directly comparable results is to measure the speed of the ships. Furthermore, the times stated in the table are only part of the story; in every case they exclude the many hours of manoeuvring which takes place between the measurement point at sea and the berth in the port.

A simple statement of the crossing time, which is intended to help the layman understand the ship's speed, is therefore misleading. For example, when we read that the *Bremen* took four days, 14 hours and 30 minutes to complete her record voyage in 1929, this does not mean her actual time between casting off in Cherbourg – not to mention Bremerhaven – to docking in New

York; it simply records the time she took to cross between the Mole of Cherbourg and the Ambrose lightship off New York, both of which were passed at full speed. The part of the trip spent steaming in and out of port at low speed, plus the time-consuming manoeuvres of docking and landing, are not included in the record times at all, though they add many hours to every crossing.

Most passengers on regular scheduled voyages were probably unaware that these record times were an unreliable guide to the duration of the open sea crossing. In our example the stated record time was achieved by running at an average speed of 27.83 knots, but the scheduled average speed of the *Bremen* was only 26.25 knots, and in reality the speed of 26.25 knots could only be maintained as an average if the ship was capable of steaming at higher speeds in order to compensate for periods of slow running due perhaps to occasional bad weather or other adverse circumstances. The high average speed could only be attained because the ship was capable of the maximum speed achieved on the record crossings.

Here is another example showing the doubtful nature of simple statements of crossing time. When the Compagnie Générale Transatlantique (CGT) and Cunard White Star agreed on a common schedule for the liners *Normandie* and *Queen Mary* in 1935, they confidently referred to the vessels as four-day ships although this was, to say the least, wishful thinking, if not actually misleading. The scheduled speed of these ships was 28.5 knots, which meant four and a half days for the journey between Cherbourg and New York.

Such a crossing hardly offered any time advantage over a five-day ship, since either the departure time or the arrival time would be inconveniently at night when it was difficult if not

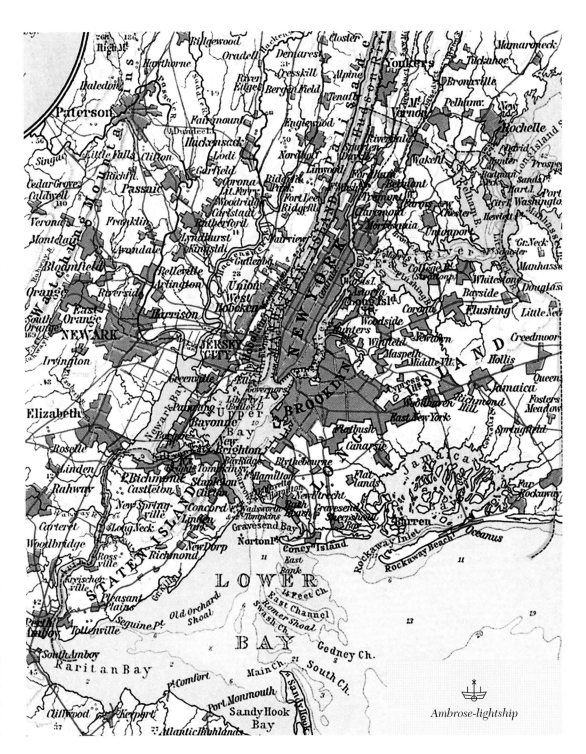

New York – shown here around 1895 – was the main destination for North Atlantic services, and after 1850 it was the destination of all Blue Riband winning ships. In every case they had already won it about 20 nautical miles previously, when they passed the island of Sandy Hook, located south of Lower Bay, or – after 1909 – the Ambrose lightship, stationed to the East of Sandy Hook. Its position is shown at bottom right.

Ambrose-lightship

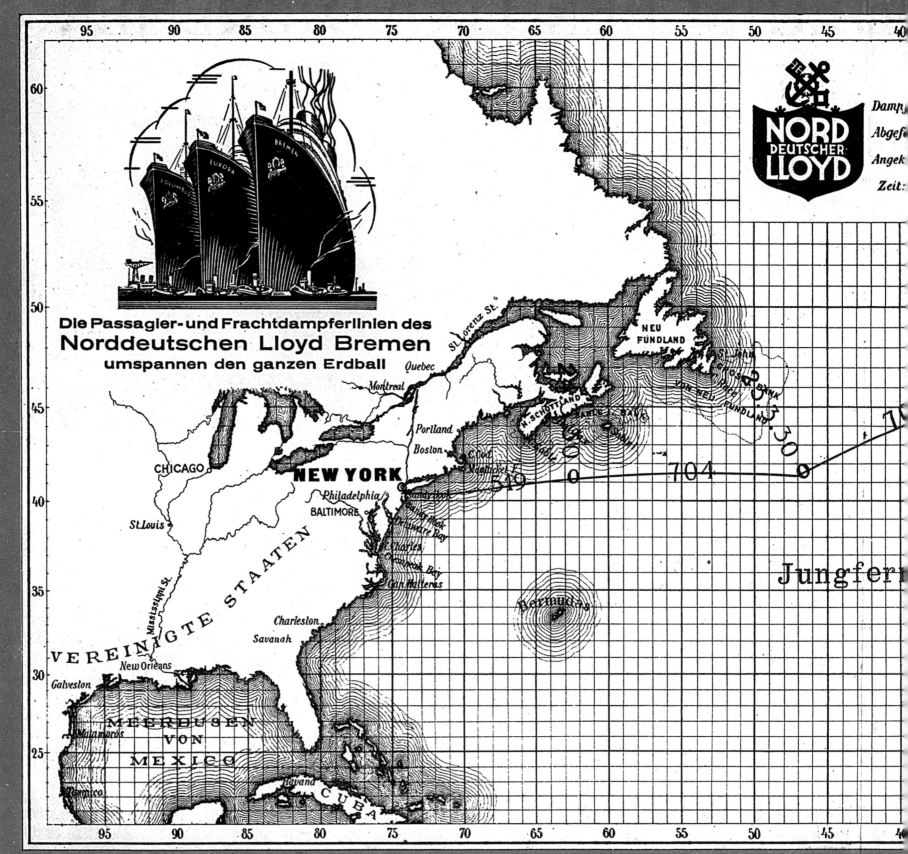

Die Passagier- und Frachtdampferlinien des
Norddeutschen Lloyd Bremen
umspannen den ganzen Erdball

NORD DEUTSCHER LLOYD

G.Hunckel, Brem

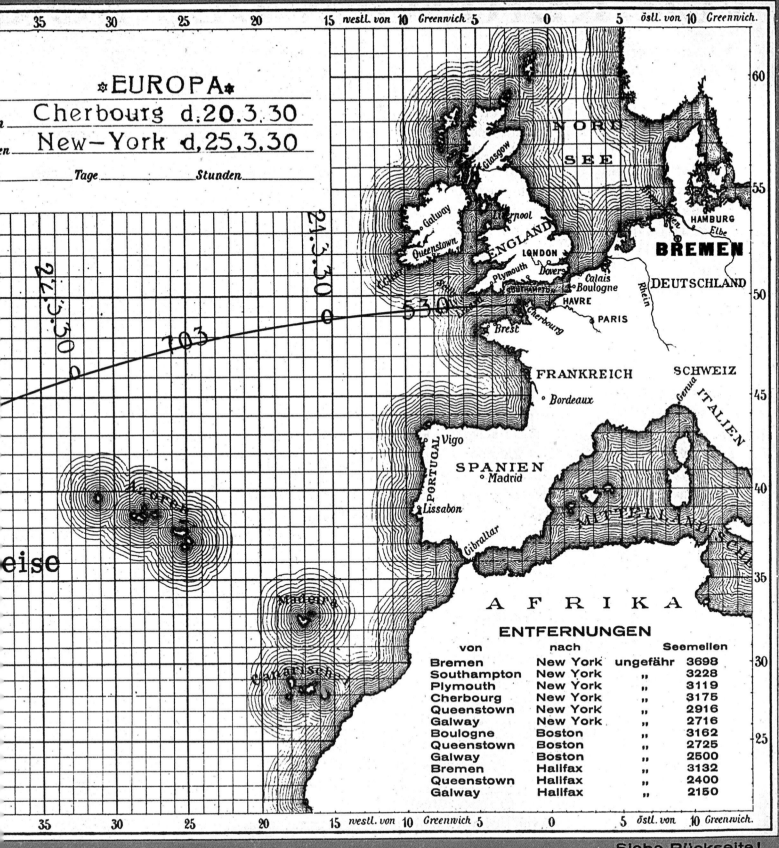

✵EUROPA✵

Cherbourg d. 20.3.30

New—York d, 25,3,30

Tage ⋯ Stunden

ENTFERNUNGEN

von	nach		Seemeilen
Bremen	New York	ungefähr	3698
Southampton	New York	„	3228
Plymouth	New York	„	3119
Cherbourg	New York	„	3175
Queenstown	New York	„	2916
Galway	New York	„	2716
Boulogne	Boston	„	3162
Queenstown	Boston	„	2725
Galway	Boston	„	2500
Bremen	Halifax	„	3132
Queenstown	Halifax	„	2400
Galway	Halifax	„	2150

Siehe Rückseite!

impossible to complete the passport or customs formalities. Neither would any form of further transport be available in the middle of the night. Nevertheless, since the shipping companies wanted to quote 'four days' in their advertising, record voyages were occasionally made at average speeds of more than 30 knots. Even at this speed the Cherbourg–New York crossing could not be completed in four days, so Cunard and the CGT simply shifted the starting point for the record run to the Bishop Rock lighthouse at the entrance to the English Channel, 190 nautical miles to the west towards New York. This made it possible to complete the crossing in just under four days, though the claim ignored the fact that the 190 nautical miles from Cherbourg to the Bishop Rock added a good six hours to the journey time, while manoeuvring off New York, including a quarantine stop, took a further five hours or so.

The second condition was that record crossings of the Atlantic only counted for the Blue Riband when carried out in the east–west direction. That is the more difficult course, as it runs

Aerial photograph of New York around 1940. In the centre the island of Manhattan, bounded by the Hudson River on the left and the East River on the right. Almost the entire southern part is hemmed in by what are known as finger piers, which are the landing places for the steamships. Without exception these piers are owned or leased by the various shipping companies. On the left of the Hudson, from bottom to top, are the areas of New Jersey, Hoboken and Weehawken, also featuring similar piers. Until 1917 both Hapag and North German Lloyd had their piers at Hoboken. In the bottom centre is Governors Island, to its right the city district of Brooklyn, where the *Bremen* and *Europa* landed their passengers in their first years of service, until 1936.

counter to the Gulf Stream and the prevailing westerly winds. In the opposite direction, from America to Europe, following winds are often encountered. A fair contest is only possible if the conditions are the same for all, so it was essential to lay down one direction for the record route. Apart from other considerations, this avoided the possibility of two ships simultaneously claiming that they held the Blue Riband. How could they have been differentiated? One option might have been to award the Blue Riband 1st class for the westbound record, and a 2nd class equivalent for the opposite direction. If one ship held both records, a further award could have been made.

Of course, setting a record in any direction is also a performance worthy of recognition. Nobody would contradict this, and such a feat can be entered in the list of record voyages in the easterly direction. Nevertheless, the Blue Riband itself–the distinction awarded to the fastest ship–was the prize in a fair competition under conditions which were as far as possible comparable. An example from athletics similarly tries to create fairness: in the 100m sprint

In 1935 the Bishop Rock lighthouse on the Scilly Isles was appointed the eastern end and final reference point of the record course.

This is how the New York quayside looked around 1907 when the *Lusitania* entered port for the first time.

The Blue Riband winner *Lusitania* arriving in New York on 13 September 1907 in New York. On the left we see the former Castle Garden theatre, which acted as the New York passenger terminal in the mid-nineteenth century.

worthy Member of Parliament for Hanley in Staffordshire. Early in life he had set himself three ambitions, and by the time in question he had already achieved two of them: he possessed a fortune of £10,000, and he was a member of the House of Commons. Hales was a former marine engineer, and his third ambition was to donate a perpetual trophy for the fastest ship. This he fulfilled in 1935 by commissioning a Sheffield goldsmith to create a silver cup of appropriate lavishness: it weighed seven stone and was nearly five feet tall. The cup was due to be completed in the summer of 1935, and by then Hales had already selected the Italian liner *Rex* to be the first holder, as she was at that time the reigning Queen of the Seas.

a new record is only valid if it is achieved without the help of a following wind above an agreed strength.

Analysis of all the arguments for and against these unwritten laws, together with a study of the information presented in the chapter describing the research and literature on the Blue Riband (see page 19), suggests that these were, indeed, the rules under which this great unofficial trophy was competed for.

THE HALES TROPHY

When the Blue Riband is the subject of conversation, Harold K Hales and his North Atlantic Blue Riband Challenge Trophy are often mentioned, and, indeed, he played an important part in the story.° In 1934 Hales was sixty-seven years old, and was the

Hales arranged with the Italian ambassador that the cup would be awarded to the *Rex* in August 1935. However, it is clear that Hales was not quite able to keep abreast of developments, otherwise he would surely have waited for the *Normandie* to complete her first crossing, as in July 1935 this ship promptly relieved the *Rex* of the Blue Riband. Hales was now in a quandary; he had promised the trophy to the Italians, but it was now the rightfully due to the French. He had to find a compromise, and his solution was to alter the conditions: any new claimant to the trophy would first have to wait three months, to give the existing holder a

---

°The information concerning Hales is based on his autobiography, Harold K Hales, *The Autobiography of 'The Card'* (London, around 1937), and in Maurizio Eliseo, *Rex* (Parma 1992)

chance to defend his record. The two parties agreed to this; initially the trophy went to the *Rex* for a period of three months, and only then was it to be transferred to the *Normandie*. However, the cup had hardly had time to reach Genoa onboard the *Rex* when a new problem arose. The *Normandie* was due for a refit starting in November, and it was considered unbecoming to award the prize amongst the deafening din of the riveting hammers at the shipyard quay, so a new compromise was found and the Italians surrendered the splendid trophy after holding it for just two months, so that it could be handed over to the new bearer in conditions of suitable splendour.

If Hales could have foreseen the fate which awaited his trophy, he might well have decided against commissioning it at all. In 1936 the *Queen Mary* won the Blue Riband, and the International Committee offered the justly earned reward to the Cunard Chairman, Sir Percy Bates. However, Bates emphatically refused the trophy, pronouncing that Cunard operated a regular scheduled service for which no trophy would be accepted, and that Cunard did not take part in any competitive races. Hales, perhaps not unreasonably affronted, had the award statutes altered again. His trophy was now to be available only to 'non-British ships'. The result was that the splendid trophy languished in a safe for a year before being re-awarded to the *Normandie*. However, in 1938, the *Queen Mary* won the Blue Riband again, which she held for the next fourteen years. Sometime during this long period the trophy managed to become mislaid, but was fortunately rediscovered in 1952, just in time to be handed over to the Americans, who had finally managed to win the Blue Riband with the *United States*.

The rules which Hales had drawn up were never really practicable. His condition that the trophy was not to be awarded to a new ship until three months after the record

crossing, to enable new vessel's predecessor the opportunity to win back the Blue Riband within that period, and therefore have a chance to keep the trophy for herself, was really nonsensical. It meant that a new record, set fairly and undisputed, could be nullified, as if the crossing had never been made. In one important respect, however, Hales' rules reflected wisdom: his silver prize was to be awarded only for the east-west crossing.

Finally, *Hoverspeed Great Britain* and her successors deserve a mention. In 1990 this vessel completed the run from Ambrose to Bishop Rock at an average speed of 37.45 knots, and since then this ship has appeared in many lists as the new holder of the Blue Riband. It is indeed a fact that the British owners of this catamaran ferry won a court judgment in their favour, and the Hales Trophy was awarded to them. But in truth, this vessel could not qualify. First, she was not a North Atlantic passenger ship. Second, she was not on a regular scheduled crossing; in fact she was crossing the North Atlantic on her transfer from the Australian dockyard to Great Britain; she carried no passengers, and on this journey they would not even have been permitted.

Last, the ship crossed the Atlantic in the easterly direction, which, as we have seen, was contrary to one of the most important qualifications for the Blue Riband.

Naturally, these objections also apply to the *Virgin Atlantic*

The Hales Trophy, donated by Harold K Hales in 1935.

When the *Kaiser Wilhelm der Grosse* became the first ship to compete for the Blue Riband via the English Channel in 1897, the Needles on the Western point of the Isle of Wight, off Southampton, were used as the Eastern reference point. This applied to this one ship only.

Aluminium catamarans made by the Australian Incat shipyard, such as the *Cat-Link V* pictured here, have taken part in the Hales Trophy competition since 1990, although – as explained in the text – this contest has nothing to do with the Blue Riband per se. In the period 19 to 23 June 1990 the *Hoverspeed Great Britain* completed the Ambrose – Bishop Rock route in three days, 7 hours and 54 minutes at an average speed of 36.6 knots. After a slight improvement to 36.65 knots set by the Spanish *Catalonia* in June 1998, the Danish *Cat-Link V* established a new record mark of 41.28 knots from 17 to 20 July 1998, taking two days, 20 hours and 9 minutes.

Challenger III powerboat belonging to the British entrepreneur Richard Branson, and to the high-speed boat belonging to the American Tom Gantry, which made the crossing in the 1980s, likewise to the record crossings made by the Italian *Destriero* in 1992 and the Danish catamaran *Cat-Link V* in 1998.

Anyhow, in 1988 the renewed interest in such record attempts did have some ramifications. The administrator of the Hales Trophy appointed new committee members, drawn from commercial maritime concerns, whose task would be to award the prize according to new criteria.° While this made sense, it had little to do with perpetuating Hales' real purpose when he donated the trophy. From whatever way it is looked at, this trophy can never be seen as synonymous with the Blue Riband. Hales' original aim was disputed even during his own lifetime, and only four out of fifty-nine victorious Blue Riband runs were

ever rewarded with this prize. In the final analysis, the Hales Trophy has to be judged for what it always was – a rather insignificant, though certainly ornate, adjunct to the final phase of the contest for the Blue Riband which by no means deserves the reverential respect with which it has sometimes been treated.

We can indulge the Hales Trophy, allow it its new purpose, and award the old-fashioned baroque cup to the modern high-tech catamarans. However, common sense and fairness must surely prevent us from equating the winning of this trophy with the gaining of the Blue Riband, if for no other reason than out of respect for the wonderful achievements of the express liners and the unwritten rules of the Blue Riband competition.

°*Transatlantic Challenger 1990*, special publication by Lloyd's List (London 1990) p5

Research and Documentation of the Blue Riband

BECAUSE the contest for the Blue Riband was never an official event, there is an almost complete lack of official archive material. The shipping companies which took part did compile lists of the voyages of their ships, and included data regarding speed or voyage duration which is more or less accurate. If a newly commissioned liner exceeded the speed of earlier ships, or undercut their crossing times, then in most cases the press published details of the achievement. This was certainly true in the ships' home ports, and detailed reports were also published in the newspapers of New York, the final destination of all the crossings. As a result, virtually the only sources of information are shipping company documents and press reports. The inevitable errors and contradictions found in the sources has been described by Noel R P Bonsor in his standard work, in which he provided plenty of examples.* We will return to this subject later.

Expert authors such as Arthur Maginnis and Henry Fry**, who wrote books on the subject of the Blue Riband competition, primarily based their works on the shipping companies' archive material and press announcements. Until 1939 their findings and the record lists they published were the basis for all subsequent books and articles about the Blue Riband, such as those by Lee and Benstead.† The statistical information which was printed and distributed in this way was considered to be proven and indisputable until the 1950s.

All this changed in 1955, when Bonsor for the first time published a critically revised list of the record Blue Riband cross-

The *Europa* at the Columbus quay in Bremerhaven in 1934; after 1927 this was the departure terminal for North German Lloyd (NDL) passenger steamers.

---

* Bonsor, Noel R P, *North Atlantic Seaway*, Vols 1-5 (Newtown Abbot 1975 – 1980). For list see Vol 5, p1866

** Maginnis, Arthur J, *The Atlantic Ferry*, (London 1892). Three expanded editions appeared before 1900.
  Fry, Henry, *The History of North Atlantic Steam Navigation*, (London 1896)

† Lee, Charles E, *The Blue Riband* (London around 1931)
  Benstead, C R, *Atlantic Ferry* (London 1936)

The bow of the *Europa* ploughing into heavy seas. Typical North Atlantic conditions.

Noel R P Bonsor, who researched the subject of the Blue Riband for several decades. His book *North Atlantic Seaway* is a standard work and represents the most important source of information on the subject.

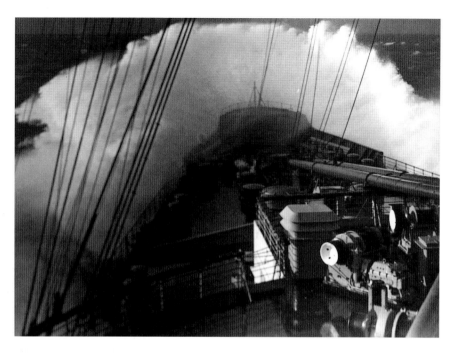

checked and in a few cases improved. The importance of these books has already been mentioned. Particularly revealing are Bonsor's numerous notes in which he analysed the source material, and his comments regarding characteristic errors and omissions in press reports and in company statements regarding the duration of Atlantic crossings, are very important. The quality of his research is indisputable.

You might, therefore, think that anyone who took an interest in the subject of the Blue Riband after about 1955 would need to read and study the standard works by Maginnis, Fry, Lee and – in particular – Bonsor, but many writers have simply not done this. It comes as a surprise to discover that many authors have ignored these important sources and perpetuated any number of fallacies and inaccuracies. This has caused widespread confusion, right to the present day; so a brief appraisal of the most important works which have appeared since 1956 is appropriate here, particularly in relation to their use of the main sources.

In 1973 a new book was published in Great Britain which set out to cover the whole history of the contest for the Blue Riband

ings*. Bonsor's account also provided, for the first time, separate lists of the record voyages in both westerly and easterly directions, and until 1975 it represented the new standard source of information on the subject. From 1975 to 1980 the new five-volume edition of Bonsor's work was published, and these books included newly revised record lists which the author had again

---

* Bonsor, Noel R P, *North Atlantic Seaway* (Prescot 1955) pp590–593

This facsimile from a brochure published in 1933 by NDL, entitled 'The Transatlantic Liners of the North German Lloyd', indicates that the Lloyd drew a clear distinction between the Blue Riband in the westerly direction, and a simple record in the easterly direction.

THE TRANSATLANTIC LINERS OF THE NORTH GERMAN LLOYD

TRANSATLANTIC RECORDS

The EUROPA is the holder of the Blue Ribbon of the Atlantic, having crossed from Cherbourg breakwater to Ambrose Lightship in March, 1930, in 4 days, 17 hours and 6 minutes. The BREMEN'S eastbound records still stand as the fastest ever made – from Ambrose Lightship to Plymouth in 4 days, 14 hours, 30 minutes — and from Ambrose Lightship to Cherbourg breakwater, 4 days, 18 hours.

The BREMEN established a new transatlantic record when she crossed from Cherbourg to Ambrose in March, 1932, in 4 days, 17 hours, 10 minutes.

A first-class cabin – French Empire style – on the White Star liner *Olympic* of 1911. White Star put luxury before speed and neither *Olympic* or *Titanic*, contrary to rumour, ever sought the Blue Riband.

Following pages. Longitudinal cross-section and the internal spaces of the German four-funnel fast steamer, using the Lloyd steamship *Kaiser Wilhelm II* as an example.

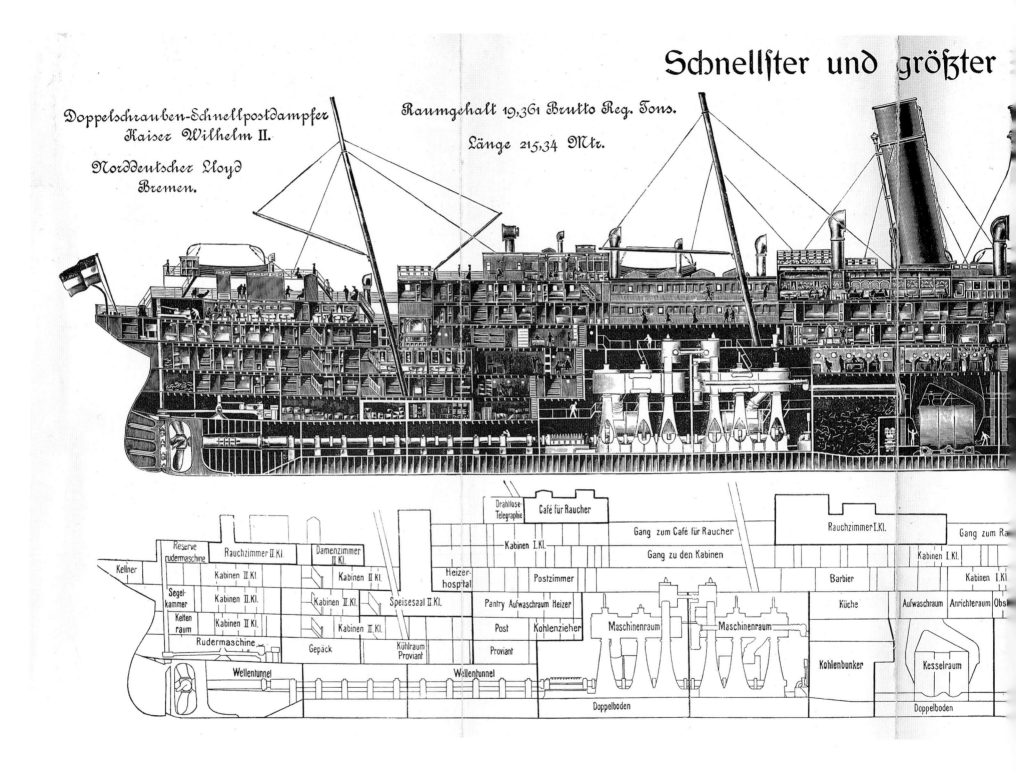

Doppelschrauben-Schnellpostdampfer
Kaiser Wilhelm II.

Norddeutscher Lloyd
Bremen.

Raumgehalt 19,361 Brutto Reg. Tons.

Länge 215,34 Mtr.

Drahtlose-Telegraphie

Café für Raucher

Gang zum Café für Raucher

Rauchzimmer I.Kl.

Gang zum Ra

Kabinen I.Kl.

Gang zu den Kabinen

Kabinen I.Kl.

Reserve rudermaschine

Rauchzimmer II.Kl.

Damenzimmer II.Kl.

Kellner

Kabinen II.Kl.

Kabinen II.Kl.

Heizer-hospital

Postzimmer

Barbier

Kabinen I.Kl.

Segelkammer

Kabinen II.Kl.

Kabinen II.Kl.

Speisesaal II.Kl.

Pantry Aufwaschraum Heizer

Maschinenraum

Maschinenraum

Küche

Aufwaschraum

Anrichteraum

Obs

Kettenraum

Kabinen II.Kl.

Kabinen II.Kl.

Post

Kohlenzieher

Rudermaschine

Gepäck

Kühlraum Proviant

Proviant

Kohlenbunker

Kesselraum

Wellentunnel

Wellentunnel

Doppelboden

Doppelboden

22

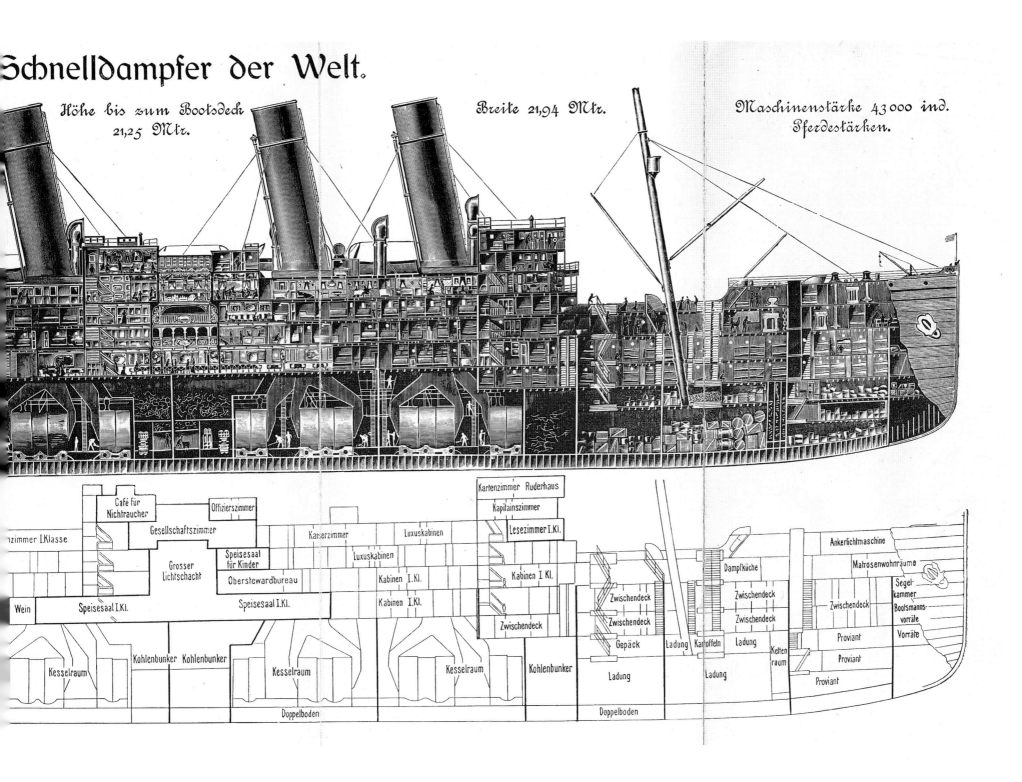

Schnelldampfer der Welt.

Höhe bis zum Bootsdeck 21,25 Mtr.

Breite 21,94 Mtr.

Maschinenstärke 43000 ind. Pferdestärken.

Café für Nichtraucher

Offizierszimmer

Kartenzimmer Ruderhaus

Kapitänszimmer

Gesellschaftszimmer

Kaiserzimmer

Luxuskabinen

Lesezimmer I.Kl.

zimmer I.Klasse

Ankerlichtmaschine

Speisesaal für Kinder

Luxuskabinen

Grosser Lichtschacht

Oberstewardbureau

Kabinen I.Kl.

Kabinen I.Kl.

Dampfküche

Matrosenwohnräume

Wein

Speisesaal I.Kl.

Speisesaal I.Kl.

Kabinen I.Kl.

Zwischendeck

Zwischendeck

Zwischendeck

Segelkammer

Kabinen I.Kl.

Zwischendeck

Zwischendeck

Zwischendeck

Bootsmannsvorräte

Gepäck

Ladung

Kartoffeln

Ladung

Vorräte

Kesselraum

Kohlenbunker Kohlenbunker

Kesselraum

Kesselraum

Kohlenbunker

Ladung

Ladung

Ketten raum

Proviant

Proviant

Proviant

Doppelboden

Doppelboden

23

Another first-class cabin on *Olympic*, this one in Old Dutch style. Historical whimsy was a distinct feature of the interior design of the liners of this era.

–the first such work since the thirties.[*] This documentary book was well researched and interestingly written by Tom Hughes, and is enlivened by many anecdotes. A German edition was published with an appendix added, which included lists of the record ships and record voyages based on Bonsor's information. This book gave the German-speaking world its first reliable source of information on the subject of the Blue Riband, and its contents were accurate according to the state of knowledge of the time.[**]

In 1980 the scientific journal of the German Maritime Museum published the first of a series of articles by myself about German express liners.[†] In these papers I dealt with the top German liners of the period 1881 to 1939 and their role in international competition. Of course, the subject of the Blue Riband arose and I took the opportunity to reflect on the unwritten rules of this contest. The results, describing the rules and regulations are laid down in the previous chapter of this book.

Many authors have attempted to see the Blue Riband competition as a reflection of the wider history of the development and culture of passenger liner operations. But the emigrant passengers, which are such a significant part of that history, for example, were certainly not a feature in the early days of the steamers before 1870. Others claim that the Blue Riband ships were synonymous with superlative levels of comfort and luxury, but the development of luxurious, cultured living on board ship took many decades, and was certainly not a noticeable apsect of the early ships. And certainly luxury was not the exclusive province of the Blue Riband ships, nor even of express liners in general. We only need to consider the North German Lloyd ships of the Fluesse class in the 1880s, which are acknowledged as the first luxury liners in the history of steam ships, but they were never the fastest Atlantic racers. From 1838 until 1899 almost all the holders of the Blue Riband were at the same time the largest

[*] Hughes, Tom, *The Blue Riband of the Atlantic* (Cambridge 1973)

[**] Hughes, Tom, *Der Kampf ums Blaue Band* [The Battle for the Blue Riband] (Oldenburg and Hamburg 1974, new edition Hamburg 1988)

[†] Kludas, Arnold, 'Die deutschen Schnelldampfer' [German express liners], parts I-V, in: *Deutsches Schiffahrtsarchiv* [German maritime archive], vols 3, 4, 6, 8 and 11, (Oldenburg and Hamburg, 1980-1988)

The luxurious Louis Seize dining room for first-class passengers in the Cunard liner *Mauretania* of 1907. For the first time on the North Atlantic *Mauretania* and her sister ship *Lusitania* offered their passengers small single tables instead of the former endless long ones.

The 46,329grt *Titanic*, built by Harland & Wolff in Belfast for the White Star Line, sank on her maiden voyage on 15 April 1912 after a night-time collision with an iceberg. Even today we occasionally read the fable that the *Titanic* had been chasing the Blue Riband on that fateful voyage, but her owners never intended her for that accolade.

The ships illustrated here were examples of large, luxuriously appointed vessels, but none of them ever won the Blue Riband. The great Isambard Kingdom Brunel designed both the *Great Britain* and the *Great Eastern*. In 1845 he delivered *Great Britain* to the Great Western Steam Ship Company, depicted here in a painting by Jochen Sachse, and at that time the 3,270grt vessel was the world's largest and most luxurious ship, and also the first screw-propelled steamer designed for overseas routes. However, with a top speed of 9 knots the ship lagged well behind the record holders of the time. The *Great Britain*, now more than 165 years old, is preserved as a museum in Bristol.

The *Great Eastern*, built in the period 1854 to 1859, displaced 18,915grt, and ranked as the largest and most comfortably appointed ship in the world by a clear margin. With her combination of paddle wheel and screw propulsion she managed 13.5 knots on her trials, and in theory this would have sufficed to win her the Blue Riband, but this speed was never achieved on the North Atlantic route. Her massive size was only just within the limits set by the technology of the time, and she only completed four years in passenger service. Thereafter, she was employed as a cable-layer, and when she entered the breaker's yard in 1888 she was still the largest ship in the world.

ships in the world. However, in terms of size and luxury they only represented the pinnacle of development until 1899, and even then there were exceptions. After this date the pre-eminent position in terms of luxury was taken by ships such as the White-Star liners *Oceanic* and *Celtic*, and the Hapag steamers *Amerika* and *Kaiserin Auguste Victoria*; the French liners *France* and *Paris* are further good examples. Between 1907 and 1911 the *Lusitania* and *Mauretania* were the largest and fastest ships on the Atlantic, but opinions on their level of comfort are more ambiguous. Certainly, from 1911 to 1935 the holders of the Blue Riband were never both the most luxurious *and* the largest ships in the world. These distinctions were claimed by other vessels, like *Titanic* and *Olympic* belonging to the White Star Line; the Hapag *Imperator*, *Vaterland* and *Bismarck*, or *Ile de France* of the Cie. Gén. Transatlantique. All these ships, from the *Celtic* in 1901 right up to *Ile de France* in 1927, and including *Kaiserin Auguste Victoria* and *Titanic*, were destined to not even participate in the contest for the Blue Riband. Rather, they represented a new strategy for the future, which did not necessarily envisage further increases in speed, and indeed, there was to be no significant increase for a period of many years. The price for any slight improvement in speed would have translated into an excessive rise in the ships' running costs. In fact, the primary selling point of these vessels was the unequivocal improvement in the level of luxury they offered, and their slightly lower speeds, combined with a reduction in noise and vibration, were fully appreciated by passengers, many of whom were quite content to stay at sea for an extra day in order to enjoy these advantages. It was not until the advent of the *Normandie* in 1935 that the Blue Riband liners once again boasted all the superlatives in terms of size, speed *and* luxury.

So the history of passenger shipping is not synonymous with the history of the Blue Riband. There are many books which make a competent job of describing North Atlantic passenger shipping, but attempts to make the Blue Riband the core or basis for such narratives have proved to be seriously flawed. It is simply not possible to stick to the essential elements of the competition for the Blue Riband and at the same time hope to tell the much wider story of transatlantic shipping.

The Contest for the Blue Riband

'EXPRESS LINERS' is the term used for ocean-going steamers which are close to the limit in terms of speed, size and passenger appointments as set by the state of the technical development of their time. Thus, the first Cunard steamers of 1840, although only capable of nine or ten knots, qualify as express steamers just as clearly as the *United States* of 1952, whose top speed was four times as fast.

Between these two extremes lies more than a century of technical invention, development and progress, and without the competition for the imaginary Blue Riband these advances would not have been implemented so quickly. Any book about the Blue Riband is bound to concentrate to some extent on one characteristic of fast steamers in particular, namely their maximum speed. No high top speed: no Blue Riband. For this reason we must at least sketch in the background of steam engine development in the period 1838 to 1952, albeit using a broad brush, for without exception all the winners of the Blue Riband were, of course, steam ships. A detailed account of these developments precedes each of the following parts covering the three great eras.

A special problem on steam ships was the working conditions of the stokers in the boiler rooms and the manual workers in the coal bunkers. On the typical large high-speed steamer these groups encompassed hundreds of men, who had to perform the most arduous labour imaginable in conditions of ceaseless heat and dust. Towards the end of each voyage the toil became harder and harder as the route from the coal bunkers to the boilers grew ever longer, because the coal located close to the boilers had by then been burned. Such exertions could only be sustained by strong, thoroughly fit men, but since their health and suitability were not examined before they were hired, tragic accidents were a regular occurrence. Men would collapse from the extreme strain, but they were nevertheless kept working, and even forced to keep working, because the foremen were responsible for maintaining the steam pressure, and replacement workers were not available at sea. Those who elected to work their passage had a grievous time too, if their task was to haul coal. These pitiable individuals did not even know what they were letting themselves in for. It was amongst this group, labouring at arduous and unfamiliar work, that many lost their sanity and took whatever course came into their minds; not a few of them suddenly ran on deck and leaped over the side in order to put an end to their wretched ordeal. Until 1914 maritime officials had to deal with dozens of such cases, year after year[*]. It was not until the advent of oil-fired boilers, which were not introduced on a large scale until after the First World War, that these almost inhuman working conditions suddenly ceased, with the result that these labourers found their employment gone, and no replacement offered.

As has already been mentioned, one effect of the Blue Riband was certainly to promote technical progress; the two most important examples will show this clearly enough. First, although envi-

Murderous toil in the boiler room.

---

[*] I describe this matter in greater detail, with many examples, in my papers on German fast steamers; see note on p25.

The flags and funnel markings of all the shipping companies which took part in the Blue Riband contest.
Drawn by J F Horst Koenig.

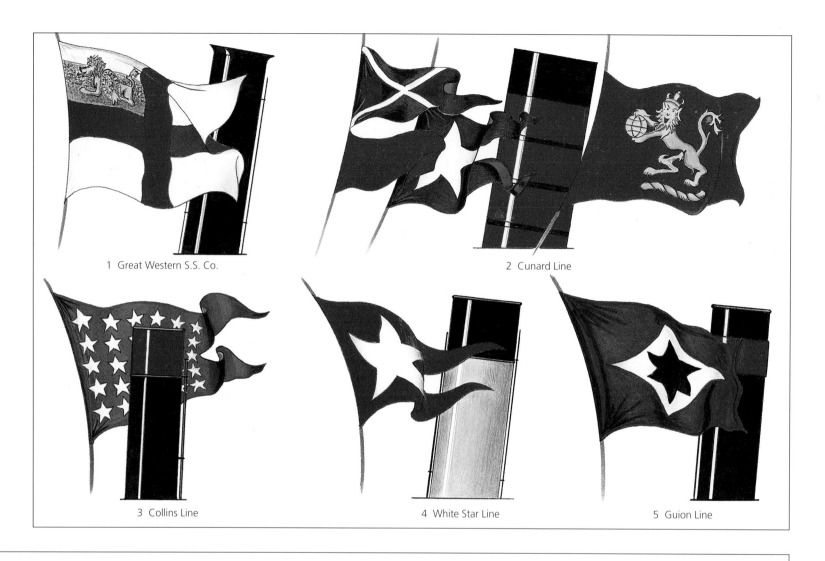

1 Great Western S.S. Co.

2 Cunard Line

3 Collins Line

4 White Star Line

5 Guion Line

NOTES: In most cases the illustrations are correct for the time when the shipping line first engaged in the competition. It is important to realise that certain elements changed in the course of time, for instance, the Cunard lion, the Lloyd funnel, the United States Lines eagle and the heraldic shield on the Hapag flag.

–Cunard: According to Bonsor the Cunard funnel marking was red with a black top prior to 1881, and lacked the characteristic black rings on the red section. However, contemporary pictures of earlier ships usually show the funnel rings (required for cable attachments and the steam whistle) black, which look like the later funnel marking. Until 1850 the blue pennant incorporating the St Andrew's cross was the company's flag, and after this time it was supplemented by a smaller red pennant. Finally, around 1880, the red flag with the golden

lion was introduced. From 1934 to 1949 the Cunard ships carried the White Star Line flag below the lion flag. The blue swallowtail flag with the white star, drawn behind the pennants, was carried by Cunard's North Atlantic ships for a brief period in the 1870s.

–White Star: the swallowtails of the flag were shortened at a later date, and after 1900 the funnel colour was approximately ochre in tone.

–Inman: the flag with the red ground was superseded in 1886 by the white one bearing the red letters I & I.

–Hapag and Lloyd: the yellow paint of the Lloyd funnel – evidently also used by Hapag – was much lighter in tone before the First World War than afterwards.

6 Inman Line

7 North german Lloyd

8 Hamburg-Amerika Linie

9 Italia Flotta Riunite

10 Cie.Gén. Transatlantique

11 United States Line

ronmental protection was not a major issue at this time, the constant improvements in the efficiency of the engine installations reduced the consumption of coal. Second, technical progress reduced costs to the point where millions of emigrants were able to afford a low-cost crossing to the New World after 1850, and in reasonably humane conditions. Instead of the sailing ship crossing, often taking six weeks or more, the steam ships took only fourteen days, thereby avoiding the onset of illnesses brought about by vitamin deficiency which had previously been such a major problem.

At this point I wish to discuss briefly the repeated claims by some that the shipping companies of the steam era shamelessly made their fortunes exploiting the emigrants, and that it was the emigrants, travelling in the steerage class, who subsidised the luxurious living to be found in First Class; a claim which is often made with specific reference to the Blue Riband itself. The arguments have been rehearsed often enough but are worth repeating here.

The long duration of the crossings on the packet sailing ships, and consequent illnesses brought about by the lack of fresh

water and food – vital vegetables would decay after four weeks, if not sooner – were most keenly felt by the emigrants.

Illness could have devastating effects in the cramped conditions on board ship. A reported mortality rate of five per cent of the passengers upon arrival in New York was considered so unremarkable that it was not deemed to deserve an announcement in the press. Yet such inhumane conditions did not escape the attention of the emigrant associations, the public at large and finally the legislators, with the result that by the middle of the nineteenth century the law had put a stop to the worst of the grievances. After 1850, when steamers began to accept passengers travelling steerage, voyages improved. Travellers now spent only two weeks at sea, and this represented an important change for the better. This was simply due to technical progress in engine technology, which in turn was promoted by the struggle to gain the Blue Riband. And while the poor emigrants in steerage experienced none of the luxury of First Class the sheer availability of berths represented previously unimagined opportunities for those seeking escape from poverty or persecution in Europe. Just as shipping companies seized the opportunity to pander to the desires of the wealthy, so they filled a need for those seeking a cheap crossing to the promised land. As the number of emigrants increased year by year, the shipping companies naturally saw a good opportunity for increasing their earnings. If they rigged a steerage facility above the holds, then they could fill it with emigrants on the out-trip to New York, and fill it with colonial goods, such as cotton, for the return crossing. Passengers' quarters in the steerage area were for a long time spartan in their simplicity, but this was due not so much to any excessive greed on the part of the shipping companies but in response to the requirements of the emigrants. The primary need of the emigrants was to reach America as cheaply as possible, and they were anxious to hold on to their money in order to gain a toe-hold in the New World. As a result the shipping companies provided them only with bed, food and drink and the simplest possible standards of sanitation. Better conditions would have translated into increased ticket prices which would have simply driven the emigrants elsewhere. The shipping companies capitalised on the huge demand for cheap travel: the emigrants were happy to have a relatively cheap and safe means of crossing the Atlantic.

The business of carrying emigrants became highly profitable, and an increasing number of new shipping companies wanted a share, with the result that conditions for the emigrants on board ship also improved. Supply and demand and competition made it all possible. For example, in an effort to attract passengers some companies began to make tin mugs and cutlery available, where before emigrants had had to supply their own. The next shipping company would then offer the steerage passengers warm woollen blankets which they could even take with them when they left the ship; soon even bedclothes were provided, as in the higher classes. The next advance was the introduction of small cabins for four or six persons, and although the furnishings were simple, this meant that a family could stay together, rather than spending the night with hundreds of other people in large dormitories. Incidentally, this 'luxury' was first offered in 1871 by the Blue Riband liners of the White Star line. As each improvement was introduced, rival shipping companies had to offer the same extras in order to keep up and retain the emigrant business. Again and again new ideas were hatched in order to attract the steerage passengers, and in most cases the emigrants had to pay no extra for these improvements, or at most a small amount. It was a highly competitive business and the way in which it developed undoubtedly brought advantages to the customer as well as to the shipping companies.

The First Era: 1819 to 1872

Paddle Steamers with Side-Lever Engines

The Propulsion Technology of Fast Paddle Steamers

UNTIL 1850 all the holders of the Blue Riband were wooden paddle steamers, a fact which might astonish today's reader. The first iron steam ship had been launched as far back as 1821, and naturally the shipping companies were aware of the advantages of iron as a construction material compared with timber. The primary ones were the relative ease of shaping iron, and the lower weight of the ships' hulls built from it, due to the greater structural strength of the metal. The companies would have welcomed the weight saving in particular, but that iron was not adopted back in 1840 was due mainly to the fact that shipbuilders were still mostly organised to build in wood and had not converted their methods to cope with the new material. Even then, it was necessary for the rolling mills to increase their capacity to keep pace with the growing demand. Emotion was probably also a factor in the slow rate of change, because timber had been the sole shipbuilding material available to man for several millennia, and shipwright and shipping company alike found it hard to abandon. Other reasons probably included the influence on Cunard's shipbuilding policy of the British Admiralty which, due to the prevailing subsidy system for mail steamers, insisted on forms of construction which were well tried and tested. On the other side of the Atlantic the Americans' shortage of iron and abundant supplies of timber prolonged the life of wooden shipbuilding.

In 1838 Isambard Brunel's *Great Western* was the first passenger steam ship to exceed the speed of another passenger steamer on the Europe-USA route, and we can therefore consider her the first winner of the Blue Riband. In that case the vessel's wooden hull, auxiliary sails, side-lever engine, low-pressure boiler and side-mounted paddle wheels represent our starting point. Without exception all steamers of the first era under discussion here were equipped with this technology.

The side-lever engine takes its name from the lever mechanism which can be seen in the drawing. This mechanism converted the vertical reciprocating movement of the piston in the cylinder into the rotary motion of the drive shaft, which was required to turn the paddle wheels. These engines were invariably of single-cylinder design, and in the early paddle steamers with which we are dealing here they were always set up in pairs alongside each other, acting on a common shaft. The shaft turned at sixteen or seventeen revolutions per minute, driving the paddle wheels on both sides of the ship. Revolving paddle wheels had been a familiar sight since 1830, but by the 1840s the paddle boards could be feathered so that they entered the water vertically,

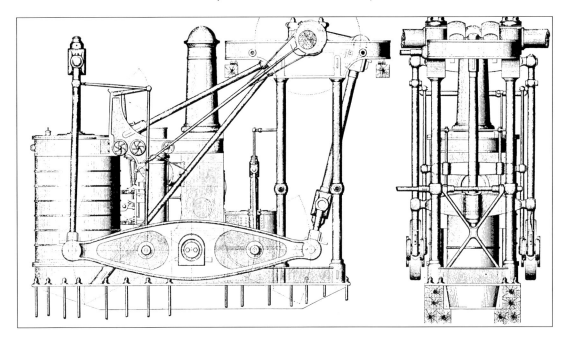

The side-lever steam engine was the most widely used power plant on the ocean-going paddle steam ships. One of the two cylinders can be seen on the left, and at top right the drive shaft for the side-mounted paddle wheels, which was operated by the side levers. The picture shows the engine of the Collins steamer *Arctic*, built in 1849.

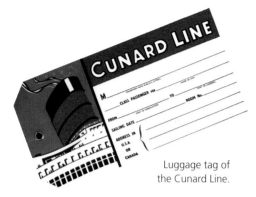

Luggage tag of
the Cunard Line.

thereby eliminating the earlier problem of the braking effect encountered with rigidly-mounted wheels. All the paddle steamers discussed in this book were equipped with this innovation.

In any discussion of steam engine technology the boilers should really take pride of place, for without the steam they produced the engines could not function at all. However, the greater technical complexity in the design of the engines themselves, and the fascination they engender in so many people – you only have to think of the incessant hissing, the innumerable moving rods, levers, wheels and shafts – have made them the most appealing aspect of steam technolgy; and bearing in mind the feeble performance of early types of boiler it is perhaps easy to understand that. The boilers installed in the first holders of the Blue Riband supplied a steam pressure of only 0.7 to 1 atmosphere ('at'; renamed 'bar' in 1977). The Collins liners of 1850 could manage 1.2at, and even the last paddle steamers built after that date operated on only slightly greater working pressure.

In the twenty years between 1851 and 1870 only two fast steamers were built which succeeded in winning the Blue Riband: the *Persia* and the *Scotia*, both belonging to the Cunard Line. Both vessels were paddle steamers, and both were propelled by the old, familiar side lever engines. This lack of progress gives some indication of the difficulties with which the engineers had to struggle in their efforts to obtain greater propulsive power.

This inability to produce higher steam pressure, meant that engineers had to concentrate on introducing all kinds of improvements to the existing engines. One simple but effective innovation was the steam jacket. This was a hollow space in the cylinder wall through which hot steam flowed, and its effect was to maintain a more even temperature in the steam cylinders, at the same time reducing the
fall in pressure which had been unavoidable in earlier engines at the point where the steam entered the non-jacketed cylinder.

Even more effective was the super-heater This was a device mounted between the boiler and the funnel in the area where the hot fumes from the furnaces were escaping; the effect was to heat the steam further, turning it into what is known as dry steam. This form of steam does not immediately suffer a fall in pressure if its temperature falls, maintaining its full working power all the way from the boiler to the engine. Dry steam is also lighter than wet steam, which meant that less steam was required to fill a cylinder, and therefore less water; this in turn was more economical on fuel. The improvement in coal consumption through the installation of super-heaters could amount to more than twenty per cent.

It was found that condensing equipment could produce an almost equally significant improvement. This was an idea which had already been invented by James Watt, but which was not incorporated into ship engine designs until around 1850. The so-called injection condenser injected seawater into the waste steam immediately after it left the cylinder, thus cooling it and liquefying it again. The resultant fall in pressure reduced the piston's internal resistance in the engine, thereby increasing available power. In the 1860s the injection condenser was in turn superseded by the surface condenser. This eliminated the highly undesirable side-effect of contamination of the boiler feed water with the seawater used to cool it. The *Scotia* incorporated all these improvements and was successful in gaining the Blue Riband in 1863; the last vessel fitted with a side lever engine and low pressure boiler to do so.

It should not be forgotten that auxiliary sail was fitted to the early steamers, and all these paddle ships were still equipped with a powerful sail plan which allowed them to sail in all conditions. Cunard had instructed his captains to set sail as often as possible, in an effort to be economical with the costly coal which fired the engines. However, this only made sense when there was a fair wind; beating to windward was obviously not to be undertaken, sails only ever being set to amplify the effect of the engines, unless an emergency occurred such as engine failure or damage to the paddle wheels. However, paddle steamers under sail were very difficult to steer due to the resistance of the wheels; the same applied to early screw-driven ships and the resistance of the propellers. Sails were also set for a quite different reason, one which the steamer captains were very appreciative of – steadying a rolling ship in a seaway; in fact, they were so effective in this role that many steamers still carried steadying sails right into the early twentieth century.

Steam Ships Conquer the Oceans

The Pioneer Years on the North Atlantic, 1819 to 1840

◆◆◆

For SEVERAL millennia there were only two possible methods of propelling a ship in a controllable manner: human muscle power, or the power of the wind. Eventually, in the eighteenth century, engineers in Great Britain, France and the USA developed steam engines, boilers and paddle wheels which could be used for the purpose of ship propulsion, and which actually proved to be feasible, practical power plants. However, it was not until the beginning of the nineteenth century that the American Robert Fulton succeeded in designing a steamer which was able to fulfil another important requirement: economy of operation. With Fulton's *Clermont* of 1807 steam navigation finally left its experimental phase; the era of industrial steam ships therefore coincided with the start of the nineteenth century. At first, the steamer captains hardly dared to set their sights beyond the river estuaries and the relative safety of coastal waters. Almost ten years were to pass before a steam ship captain boldly plotted a course aiming for the far side of the Atlantic.

The idea of records and speed contests could hardly have been in the minds of the captains and shipping companies which operated the first ocean-going steamers. If their ship arrived at its destination more or less safely, that would have seemed adequate compensation for the considerable risk incurred, and the first of the 'transatlantic steamers', the legendary *Savannah*, provides ample evidence of this claim.

THE SAVANNAH

The Savannah Steam Ship Company was founded on 7th May 1818 in Savannah, in the State of Georgia, and among the group of businessmen who were involved Moses Roger played a special role; his qualifications included many years' experience as a

steamer captain, including command of Fulton's *Clermont*. The new company was planning an ambitious project: the establishment of the first steamer line for crossing the North Atlantic. Roger purchased a sailing ship then under construction in New York, and the vessel was launched on 22 August as the *Savannah*. The ship was then fitted out with a steam engine and paddle wheels, but so many technical problems arose that the work was not completed until February 1819. During this period the company's directors evidently came to the realisation that the

In 1819 the *Savannah* was the first steam ship to cross the North Atlantic, and therefore ranks as the world's first ocean-going steamer.

Only four days after the *Sirius*, the *Great Western* set off for New York and managed to beat the speed of the earlier vessel; she can be reasonably regarded as the first winner of the Blue Riband.

Profile of the *Great Western* of 1838.

Profile of the *Sirius* of 1837.

Savannah could never be suitable for the planned service as a liner. At 320 gross registered tons (grt) the ship required almost all its hold capacity simply to accommodate the bunker coal. Once the ship had been transferred to her home port of Savannah, the company attempted in vain to sell her to the US Navy, and even before her maiden voyage rumours of her impending sale to Russia were circulating.

On 22 May 1819, when the *Savannah* finally set off on her voyage to Liverpool, she carried neither load nor passengers– not one of the thirty-two passenger berths had been booked– so Captain Moses Roger and his crew set out to sea with just 75 tons of coal and a supply of firewood. Right from the outset the fuel supply was meted out with the greatest care, and the power of the wind was used whenever possible. On 17 June the *Savannah* was spotted from the Irish coast at Cape Clear. As great clouds of smoke were visible the alarm went out that the ship was on fire and the British cutter *Kite* was commanded to sail out to cope with an emergency at sea. However, by this time the fire under the boilers was almost extinguished due to lack of coal, and Captain Roger was obliged to head for the port of Kinsale to fill up his bunkers. From there to the Mersey it was little more than a stone's throw, and on 20 June the ship anchored off Liverpool. This first Atlantic crossing under steam had lasted twenty-nine days and 11 hours, but in strict terms the voyage could hardly be termed to have taken place 'under steam power' for the ship had spent more time under sail than other-wise. Only on twelve days had steam been raised, and then usually only for a few hours. In total the *Savannah* had steamed for only about 90 hours out of a total of 707 hours spent at sea. Although the crossing clearly showed that a regular line service with steam ships was still a long way in the future, the nautical and technical achievement of Captain Moses Roger must still rank as a remarkable pioneering feat, and the fact that fourteen years were to pass before a second passenger steamer made a successful attempt at the long voyage across the Atlantic only goes to emphasise the achievement.

THE *ROYAL WILLIAM*

The *Royal William* was another vessel which crossed the Atlantic only once. The notable feature of this voyage was that the ship carried paying passengers across the Atlantic for the first time under steam power. Originally, the Quebec & Halifax Steam Navigation Company had built their ship in 1831 for the route between Quebec, Halifax and Pictou, but the results of a cholera epidemic caused the steamer's first year of service to suffer such heavy financial losses that the owners decided to sell her, and on 18 August the steamer set off from Pictou to cross the Atlantic. The ship carried seven paying guests, and the crossing was extremely stormy, but even so the propulsion system proved satisfactory in spite of a temporary failure in the starboard engine. Every four days the fires under the boilers had to be put out for about 24 hours, so that salt crystals could be removed from the boilers. After a voyage lasting twenty-two days Captain McDougall successfully anchored the *Royal William* in the Solent off Cowes.

The *Royal William*, drawn by Frank O Braynard.

The Sirius and the Great Western

As we have seen, the first two transatlantic voyages by passenger steamers were the direct result of economic necessity, namely, that the owners needed to sell the uneconomic ships, the prospects for which appeared better in Europe. It is true that plans for a regular steam ship service across the Atlantic had been considered back in the 1820s, but the technical realities of the day doomed them to failure°. The simple truth was that the steam engine had not yet reached a sufficient stage of development to make it suitable for long ocean voyages.

In 1835, an American living in London, Dr Junius Smith, announced publicly that he planned to found a steam ship line running to New York. This idea had come to him during a sailing ship voyage across the Atlantic which lasted 57 days; such jour-

ney times were by no means rare at that time. If the current state of technology could be harnessed correctly, so Smith thought, it should be possible to put an end to such long voyages. Smith won the support of experienced businessmen, and raised the capital for the London-based British & American Steam Navigation Company. The company placed an order for a steam ship of 1900grt, which was several times larger than any previous vessel of the type. Unfortunately, the company contracted to build the engines went bankrupt, delaying the completion of *British Queen* by several months, and this might have proved fatal as competition was already stirring in Bristol at the time, and the British & American ran the danger of being overtaken. Fortunately, the directors of the shipping company had good

°Cf Bonsor, Noel R P; *North Atlantic Seaway*, vol. 1, chapters 3 and 4.

ss *Savannah*	ss *Royal William*	ss *Sirius*	ss *Great Western*
Owner: Savannah Steam Ship Company, Savannah.	*Owner*: Quebec & Halifax Steam Navigation Company.	*Owner*: British & American Steam Navigation Company, London.	*Owner*: Great Western Steamship Company, Bristol.
Builder: Samuel Ficket & William Crocket, New York.	*Builder*: Black & Campbell, Quebec.	*Builder*: Robert Menzies & Son, Leith.	*Builder*: William Patterson, Bristol.
Specification: 320grt / 110ft overall length / 25.8ft beam, 36ft across wheel cases/one horizontal single-cylinder low-pressure steam engine by Dod, Vail & Allaire / 90ihp / two side paddle wheels / 4 knots / thirty-two passengers in cabins.	*Specification*: Approx 500grt / 176ft overall length / 28ft beam / two horizontal single-cylinder low-pressure steam engines; Bennet & Henderson / two side paddle wheels / 7 knots / passengers in cabins / crew of thirty-six.	*Specification*: 703grt / 200ft registered length / 25ft beam / one two-cylinder side lever steam engine; Wingate & Co. / 600ihp / two side paddle wheels / 7.5 knots / passengers in cabins / crew of thirty-six.	*Specification*: 1340grt / 235ft overall length / 35.25ft beam, 58ft across wheel cases / one two-cylinder side lever steam engine / Maudslay, Sons & Field / 750ihp / two side paddle wheels / 8.5 knots / 128 passengers, first-class; twenty servants' berths in foreship.
Career: 1818 laid down as packet sailing ship for Le Havre service; purchased before completion / 22.8.1818 launched / 2.1819 trials / 28.2.1819 delivery voyage New York–Savannah / 22.5. to 20.6.1819 maiden crossing Savannah–Liverpool / steam demonstration runs to Helsingoer, Stockholm and St. Petersburg, then under sail to Copenhagen, Arendal and finally back across the Atlantic / 30.11.1819 arrived Savannah / 1821 to Nathan A. Holdridge, New York. Engine removed, employed as sailing ship between New York and Savannah / 5.11.1821 stranded off Fire Place on Long Island.	*Career*: 27.4.1831 launched / 24.8.1831 maiden voyage Quebec–Halifax / 18.8 to 9.9.1833 transatlantic crossing Pictou–Cowes / 9.1833 sold in London to Portuguese government / 10.9.1834 to the Spanish government as *Ysabel Segunda* / 1837 engine installation removed, laid up as hulk in Bordeaux.	*Career*: 1837 delivered to St. George Steam Packet Company, London. Employed on London–Cork service / 28.3.1838 start of first crossing London–New York under charter to British & American Steam Navigation Company / two round trips, then again London–New York service for the St. George Steam Packet Company / 16.1.1847 stranded off Ballycotton, Ireland, lost. Twenty dead.	*Career*: 19.7.1837 launched / 24.3.1838 trials / 31.3.1838 delivered / 8.4. to 23.4.1838 maiden voyage Bristol–New York, winning the Blue Riband; speed raised to more than 10 knots in succeeding years / 1839 to 1840 extension of aft section, additional berths. 252ft overall length, 1700grt / 1842 entered Liverpool / 1843 Liverpool–New York service / 12.1846 laid up in Liverpool after forty-five round voyages / 24.4.1847 to Royal Mail Steam Packet Company, Liverpool / 1855 transport vessel in Crimean War / 10.1856 to London, broken up.

relations with the St. George Steam Packet Company, and were able to charter its new ship, the *Sirius*, a vessel of 703grt.

On 28 March 1838 the *Sirius* left the port of London under Captain Roberts, heading for Cork, where on 4 April she embarked 450 tons of bunker coal and 20 tons of fresh water. With ninety-four passengers and a crew of thirty-seven – including one stewardess – she then put to sea making for New York. In spite of stormy weather and problems with the jittery crew the voyage was completed successfully. *Sirius* completed the crossing at an average speed of more than eight knots, and on 23 April 1838 the ship anchored off the Hudson Battery after a voyage lasting 18 days and 14 hours.

A few hours later onlookers were rubbing their eyes in disbelief. From the direction of the open sea there came another steamer, which was soon recognised as the *Great Western* belonging to the Great Western Steam Ship Company, the rival ship from Bristol. The crew of the *Sirius* could scarcely believe that she could have so quickly caught up with them; after all, the *Great Western* had still been on trials when they had passed her on the Thames in March. It turned out, however, that the *Great Western* had completed the crossing at 8.66 knots, and had thus beaten the *Sirius*. The *Great Western* was a product of the ingenious mind of that great engineer Isambard Kingdom Brunel who was to design the revolutionary *Great Britain* of 1845, and ten years later build the largest ship of its time, the *Great Eastern*.

This date, 23 April 1838, can reasonably be considered to have witnessed the inauguration of the 'Blue Riband', although at that time the term would have meant nothing to the sailors; at that early date nobody had even conceived of a contest, unofficial or otherwise. None the less, the facts are clear: the *Great Western*, a passenger ship on North Atlantic line service, exceeded the speed of another North Atlantic liner for the first time, in the same direction of travel, from Europe to North America.

This record emphasised a further point, which later proved to be an important stimulus to the building of ever faster and larger ships. *Sirius*, at 700grt, had carried more than ninety persons, while the much larger *Great Western* (1340grt) bore only seven passengers, fifty more having cancelled their bookings after they

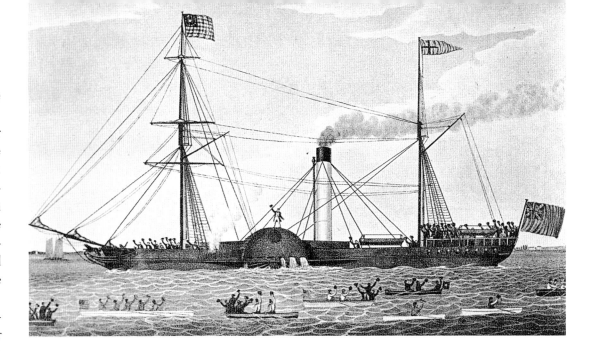

The British *Sirius* completed the crossing from Liverpool to New York in 1838, becoming the first steam ship to operate a transoceanic passenger service.

heard that the steamer had run aground on a sand bank whilst steaming to Bristol, after a relatively harmless fire in her engine room. The successful voyage changed all this, and passengers now crowded onto the larger and faster *Great Western*. In contrast, the *Sirius* had to be removed from the schedule after one further voyage, due simply to lack of passengers. A record-breaking voyage, therefore, was quick to pay a commercial dividend.

The success of the technology used on the pioneer steamers had attracted the attention of the British Admiralty, which saw that this new mode of transport promised a significant improvement in postal services between the Old and New Worlds. In November 1838 the Admiralty announced a subsidised steamer mail service, a prize which the pioneering shipping companies were keen to win. However, it was not either of these companies that were successful, but a newcomer, an interloper from Canada, one Samuel Cunard. With the acceptance of his tender the Admiralty effectively pronounced a verdict of death on both shipping companies – even though that was not its intention – for they were unable to compete against a subsidised shipping line. It was simply impossible for them to make up for the huge advantage which the subsidy represented. Both shipping companies lost ships shortly afterwards, and their days were then numbered. The British & American failed in 1841 and the Great Western in 1846.

Subsidies Smooth the Way

The Cunard Line 1841 to 1850

◆◆◆

In 1840 Samuel Cunard (1787-1865) initiated the first trans-Atlantic line service using steam ships.

SAMUEL CUNARD was a merchant from Halifax, Nova Scotia, and owner of several sailing ships. He travelled to England to put in a tender for the mail service and on 4 July 1839 signed his name on a contract which bound him to send one steam ship across the Atlantic every fourteen days in both directions between Liverpool and Halifax, and also to Boston, starting in June 1840. His first ship, *Britannia*, was to be measured at 1100grt and have a speed of 9 knots. For providing this service Cunard was to be granted an annual payment of £60,000.

What was the situation in the maritime world of the 1830s when this contract was signed? It was, in fact, a time of unprecedented mutually beneficial technical, economic and political development. The turbulent Napoleonic period in Europe had given way to an era of consolidation, and in the New World what became known as the era of unlimited possibilities had begun. With the invention of the steam engine mankind had opened up an entirely new perspective on the world's potential for development; steam engines were improving productivity to undreamed-of levels, and were revolutionising transport. The first railways were being

Charles Dickens' cabin on the *Britannia*.

built, and the first steamers were bending to their task of breaking the monopoly of the sailing ship which had existed for thousands of years.

For the first time it made sense to speak of a world economy, of a genuine exchange of the products of different continents. This vast growth in economic activity demanded a corresponding increase in lines of communication, and it became clear that the conventional merchant fleets, which combined trade and passenger transport in a single system, could not begin to cope. The first change was the formation of modern shipping companies as we know them today. At the same time marine engineers were beginning to design competent, seaworthy steam ships which offered the huge advantage of independence from the wind. In other words, journey times could be calculated and schedules drawn up which companies were able to adhere to.

Such reliable communication was what a world economy needed. It was now possible at least to aim at obtaining short mail delivery times between continents, as had already been achieved on overland routes. At that time, with neither radio, fax nor E-mail in existence, long-range communications, so vital for

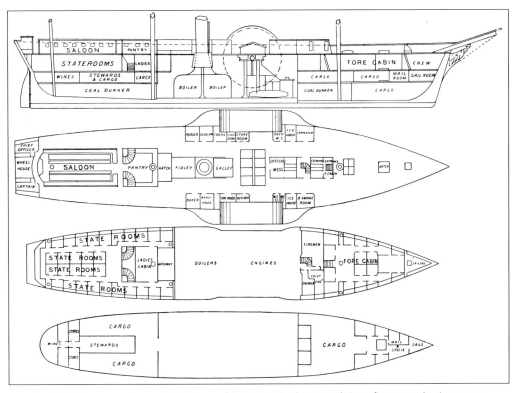

Longitudinal cross-section and deck plans of the *Britannia*, the Cunard Line's first transatlantic steamer.

very short intervals was too expensive to be viable commercially. However, if the private calculation of economic viability could not provide an answer, a political solution could be found. Such a solution was in the hands of governments and all governments still keep it in reserve for times of emergency: the expedient political subsidy. Today the term has a primarily negative connotation, but it is simply a taxation instrument without which even a free market economy cannot manage. That was precisely the aim of the Admiralty in this case.

Cunard tackled his task in a professional manner. Even before the contract was signed, he held discussions with Robert Napier, one of the leading British shipbuilders and engineers of the time, and delegated to him the design and construction of the ships. Napier's own company built the engines of the paddle steamers, while he sub-contracted the construction of the timber ships to various Scottish yards.

trade transactions, were only possible by letter. A sailing ship took up to ten weeks to cross the Atlantic, but steamers were now able to complete the stretch between Bristol and New York in as little as fourteen days. Unfortunately, there was a catch which was that operating a regular, scheduled steamer service at

By this time Cunard had registered his shipping company as the British & North American Royal Mail Steam Packet Company, a name as sonorous as it is long-winded. On 4 July 1840 *Britannia* steamed out of Liverpool, the first Cunard

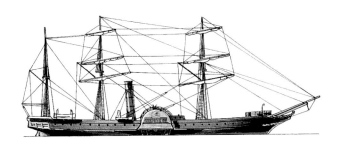

Profile of the *Cambria* of 1844.

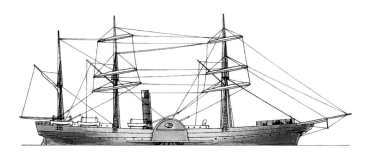

Profile of the *Europa* of 1848.

Profile of the *Columbia* of 1840.

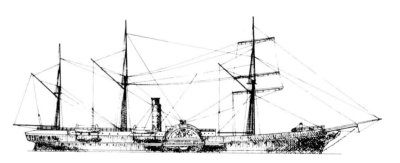

Profile of the *Asia* of 1850.

Profile of the *America* and *Europa* of 1848.

steamer, and a further three sister ships were commissioned that same year. In terms of speed, the four steamers were a fairly close match for the rival *Great Western*, which managed to compete successfully until 1843, and it was only *Columbia*, under the command of Captain Ewing, which was able to wrest the Blue Riband from her in 1841 for a period of just two years. Both *Britannia* and *Columbia* each held the record briefly for the easterly voyage.

Cunard's sole contract obligation was to deliver the mail punctually; what he did with his ships otherwise was his business, and

ss *Britannia*

Owner: Cunard Line, Liverpool.

Builder: Robert Duncan, Greenock.

Specification: 1135 grt / 230ft overall length / 34ft beam / one two-cylinder side-lever steam engine; Napier / 740 ihp / two side paddle wheels / 9 knots / 115 first-class passengers.

Career: 5.2.1840 launched / 4.7.1840 maiden voyage Liverpool–Halifax–Boston / On the return trip the ship set a record at an average speed of almost 11 knots / 18.11.1848 last transatlantic crossing / 3.1849 to German Federal Fleet and renamed *Barbarossa*, frigate / 6.6.1852 to the Prussian Navy, barracks ship in Danzig / 1865 engines

removed, barracks hulk at Kiel / 5.5.1880 decommissioned / 28.7.1880 target ship, sunk by torpedo from training ship *Zieten*. Wreck later raised and broken up in Kiel.

ss *Columbia*

Owner: Cunard Line, Liverpool.

Builder: Robert Steele & Son, Greenock.

Specification: 1175 grt / 230 overall length / 34ft beam / one two-cylinder side-lever steam engine; Napier / 740ihp / two side paddle wheels / 9 knots / 115 first-class passengers.

Career: 9.1840 launched / 5.1.1841 maiden voyage Liverpool-Halifax-Boston / 4.6. to 15.6.1841 won Blue Riband at 9.78 knots / 4.1843 *Columbia* broke record for easterly crossing at more than 11 knots, taking over from sister ship *Britannia* / 2.7.1843 stranded near Cape Sable off Nova Scotia.

ss *Hibernia*

Owner: Cunard Line, Liverpool.

Builder: Robert Steele & Son, Greenock.

Specification: 1423 grt / 240ft overall length / 37ft beam / one two-cylinder side-lever steam engine; Napier / 1040ihp / two side paddle wheels / 9 knots / 120 first-class passengers / crew 90.

Career: 8.9.1842 launched / 19.4.1843 maiden voyage Liverpool–Halifax-Boston / 1843 two record crossings in westerly direction / 1850 to Spanish Navy as *Habanois*.

any profit, if he were successful, was his. Since the steam engines of the time were so inefficient, most of the space on these small ships was taken up by coal bunkers, but Napier still managed to find space for 115 first-class passengers. The term 'First Class' is deceptive here; it implies luxury, and certainly the Cunard ships were luxurious by the standards of their day. Bearing in mind the conditions which were usual on ships around 1840, the passengers were certainly accommodated in comfort and looked after to first-class standards, even if certain contemporary intellectuals viewed things in a different light. Charles Dickens, for example – probably the most famous passenger on the first Cunard steamers – described his cabin as 'an entirely impracticable, thoroughly hopeless, and profoundly preposterous box.' Compared to the comforts of land these early ships were uncomfortable, damp and cramped, and for the conditions of the North Atlantic they were small and pitched and rolled unmercifully. Dickens was badly seasick and was largely comatose for about ten days.

Such luxury as it was had to be paid for, and perhaps that is why Dickens was so testy. As a result the first steamers made absolutely no provision for carrying emigrants, based on the

The paddle-wheel steamers *America* and *Europa*.

undoubted estimation that this category of persons would not be able to afford it. For this reason third-class passengers were still directed towards the 'tween decks of the sailing ships; eventually, by the late 1840s, some of these travellers found themselves able

ss *Cambria*	ss *America*	ss *Europa*	ss *Asia*
Owner: Cunard Line, Liverpool.	*Owner*: Cunard Line, Liverpool.	*Owner*: Cunard Line, Liverpool.	*Owner*: Cunard Line, Liverpool.
Builder: Robert Steele & Son, Greenock.	*Builder*: Robert Steele & Son, Greenock.	*Builder*: John Wood, Port Glasgow.	*Builder*: Robert Steele & Son, Greenock.
Specification: 1423grt / 240ft overall length / 37ft beam / one two-cylinder side-lever steam engine; Napier / 1040ihp / two side paddle wheels / 9 knots / 120 first-class passengers / crew 90.	*Specification*: 1825grt / 270ft overall length / 38ft beam / one two-cylinder side-lever steam engine; Napier/1400ihp / two side paddle wheels / 10 knots / 140 first-class passengers.	*Specification*: 1834grt / 270ft overall length / 38ft beam / one two-cylinder side-lever steam engine; Napier / 1400ihp / two side paddle wheels / 10 knots / 140 first-class passengers.	*Specification*: 2227grt / 290ft overall length / 40ft beam / one two-cylinder side-lever steam engine; Napier / 2000ihp / two side paddle wheels / 12 knots / 130 first-class, 30 second class passengers / crew 112.
Career: 1.8.1844 launched / 4.1.1845 maiden voyage Liverpool – Halifax – Boston / 19. to 29.7.1845 won Blue Riband at 10.71 knots / 1.1.1848 first voyage Liverpool – New York / 3.1854 troop transport in Crimean War / 29.3.1856 Liverpool – Halifax – Boston service again / 1856 chartered for Marseille – Malta service / 1860 sold to Italy.	*Career*: 13.5.1847 launched / 15.4.1848 maiden voyage Liverpool – Halifax – New York / 3. to 12.6.1848 won Blue Riband at 11.71 knots / 7.1863 to 3.1864 Liverpool – Montreal service under charter to Allan Line / 1866 first voyage Liverpool – Le Havre / 1886 *Coalgacondor*, refited as sailing ship / 1875 broken up.	*Career*: 22.9.1847 launched / 15.7.1848 maiden voyage Liverpool – Halifax – Boston, later also to New York / 13. to 23.10.1848 won Blue Riband at 11.79 knots / 27.6.1849 collided with emigrant sailing ship *Charles Bartlett*, which sank with 135 men / 1854 troop transport in Crimean War / 3.2.1866 Liverpool – Halifax – Boston service again / 1867 sold for refit as sailing ship.	*Career*: 31.1.1850 launched / 18.5.1850 maiden voyage Liverpool – Halifax – Boston, won Blue Riband at 12.25 knots / subsequent voyages mostly to New York / 1867 sold and refitted as sailing ship / 1883 broken up.

The *Columbia* of 1841.

time the company began to replace its first-generation vessels. For this improvement in performance the company was rewarded by the Admiralty which now granted an annual subsidy of £173,340. This new arrangement also included an Admiralty requirement that the ships should be prepared to be commissioned as military transports, so the extra funds were used to install gun platforms and bases. These new steamers, measuring 1800grt, were still paddle steamers of timber construction, in technical terms little more than enlarged versions of the *Britannia* of 1840. Two of these vessels, *America* and *Europa*, succeeded in winning the Blue Riband in 1848, while the *Canada* achieved a easterly record in 1849. However, since 1843 these record voyages had had little impact for propaganda purposes, for since overcoming the challenge of the *Great Western* Cunard held a practical monopoly for high-speed crossings.

to pay the more affordable prices charged for the much shorter and pleasanter steamer crossing. For the time being, though, Cunard's bookings were all from the well-heeled.

In 1843 and 1845 Cunard introduced two slightly larger ships to his line; these were *Cambria* and *Hibernia*, both of which broke existing records, although only *Cambria* won the Blue Riband while *Hibernia* steamed east.

In 1848 the four ships of the *America* class allowed the Cunard company to schedule alternating departures to New York, Boston and Halifax at shorter intervals, and at the same

After ten years of dominance, however, the Cunard company found itself facing serious competition, and its response was to make a great leap forward. In 1850 the sister ships *Asia* and *Africa* were commissioned, both of 2226grt. In the same year the *Asia* crossed the Atlantic at an average speed of 12.25 knots to win the Blue Riband for her owner. However, this was Cunard's last contender in the matter of speed for several years, and the company was obliged to accept a new position as underdog.

Robert Napier (1791-1876), whose reliable side-lever steam engine represented an important foundation for regular scheduled overseas voyages.

Around the end of the 1860s the saloon on all liners looked like the one depicted here, although, of course, there were minor variations in fittings and levels of comfort. It was located in the aftership and served as a drawing-room or saloon. At mealtimes the tables were covered, and the backrests of the upholstered benches folded back towards the gangway, converting the saloon into a dining-room. The curtains on both sides of the saloon cover the corridors along which passengers had access to their cabins.

The American Challenge

The Collins Line, 1850 to 1854

Edward K Collins (1802-1878), founder of the successful American Collins Line.

THE United States of America were connected to the Cunard Line mail service via Boston, but for a number of reasons this situation was considered by Americans to be unsatisfactory. For one thing, Boston was only the second port of call after Halifax, so the Americans received their mail a full day later than the British Canadians. Second, although Boston was an important seaport, the actual hub of the American economy was New York, and the preference shown by the British towards the New England states caused a certain irritation. The USA was one of the world's most powerful countries, and could surely afford its own mail steamer line. The US Postmaster General shared this view, and in October 1845 invited tenders for mail steamer services from New York to various European ports.

Approval for one line was granted to Edward Knight Collins, who had been running packet sailing ships between New York and Liverpool since 1836. His tender was finally accepted on 3 March 1847, although an earlier application from him in 1846 had been turned down. His New York & Liverpool United States Mail Steamship Company was to initiate a service every fourteen days between New York and Liverpool in return for an annual

The tragic sinking of the *Arctic*, which began Collins' downfall.

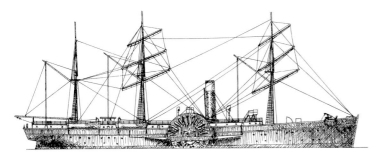

Profile of *Pacific* of 1850.

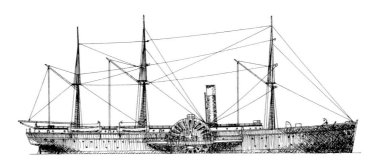

Profile of *Baltic* of 1850.

subsidy of 385,000 US dollars; in the four winter months his obligation was reduced to monthly crossings. From the outset it was agreed that this service should be faster than any other, with the result that an unusual amount of time and effort was invested in the planning and design of the four ships ordered. Collins was a progressive thinker, and would gladly have ordered iron ships, but the material was in short supply in the USA at that time, American shipbuilders did not rate it highly and so Collins was finally obliged to content himself with wooden paddle steamers.

Even so, when the *Atlantic* set out on her maiden voyage

under Captain West on 27 April 1850, she was one of the largest liners of her time, and her fixtures and fittings were of such a high level that they eclipsed the competition. Glazed ventilator ducts provided light and fresh air in the cabins, and servants could quickly be called upon via electric bells, as confirmed admiringly in contemporary reports. Unfortunately, the owners' hopes for a record crossing came to nothing when the paddle wheels were damaged by drift-ice.

Company officials at Cunard no doubt received this news with a mixture of pleasure and sorrow, for it cleared the way for the

ss *Pacific*	ss *Arctic*	ss *Baltic*	
Owners: Collins Line, New York.	*Owner*: Collins Line, New York.	*Owner*: Collins Line, New York.	charter voyages for North American Lloyd from New York–Bremerhaven / 21.2.1867 first of five charter voyages for New York & Bremen Steam Ship Co from New York–Bremerhaven / 1867 laid up / 1870 engines removed / 1880 broken up.
Builder: Jacob Bell, New York.	*Builder*: Wm. H. Brown, New York.	*Builder*: Jacob Bell, New York.	
Specification: 2707grt / 295ft overall length / 45ft beam / one two-cylinder side-lever steam engine; Allaire Iron Works / 2000ihp / two side paddle wheels / 12 knots / 200 first-class passengers / crew 145.	*Specification*: 2856grt / 298ft overall length / 45.9ft beam / one two-cylinder side lever steam engine; Novelty Iron Works / 2000ihp / two side paddle wheels / 12 knots / 200 first-class passengers / crew 145.	*Specification*: 2723grt / 296.5ft overall length / 45ft beam / one two-cylinder side-lever steam engine; Allaire Iron Works / 2000ihp / two side paddle wheels / 12 knots / 200 first-class passengers / crew 145.	
Career: 1.2.1849 launched / 25.5.1850 maiden voyage New York–Liverpool / 11. to 21.9.1850 won Blue Riband at 12.46 knots / 5.1851 record voyage in easterly direction / 1851 cabins for 80 second-class passengers installed / 23.1.1856: left Liverpool with 186 persons on board, but never reached New York. Assumed to have foundered in midatlantic.	*Career*: 28.1.1850 launched / 27.10.1850 maiden voyage New York–Liverpool / 1851 cabins for 80 second-class passengers installed / 2.1852 record voyage in easterly direction / 27.9.1854 sunk after collision with French steamer *Vesta* South of Cape Race. 332 dead, 59 rescued.	*Career*: 5.2.1850 launched / 16.11.1850 maiden voyage New York–Liverpool / 6. to 16.8.1851 won Blue Riband at 12.91 knots / 1851 cabins for 80 second-class passengers installed / 2.1858 laid up in New York / 9.7.1859 to North Atlantic Steam Ship Co, New York. New York–Aspinwall service / 1860 laid up / 1861 transport ship in American Civil War / 26.4.1866 first of two	

A contemporary oil painting of *Atlantic*. This was the first ship of the Collins Line, and set a new record in 1851 in the easterly direction.

new *Persia* to gain the Blue Riband unchallenged in May 1850, and she was even able to defend it for a few months. However, Collins very soon proved to the British that there was no denying competition. In September 1850, once the engineers had run-in the engines of the Collins liners, the *Pacific* succeeded in relieving the *Asia* of the Blue Riband. In the following year the Collins liner *Baltic* assumed the lead, and she was able to extend her advantage in 1854. Also in the easterly direction Collins' ships were successful. The *Pacific* set a new record for this route in May 1851, before being surpassed in turn by her sister ship the *Arctic* in 1852. On these record crossings the vessels' coal consumption rose to heights which were certainly uneconomic; for their standard service speed of twelve knots alone around 90 tons of fuel had to be fed to the boilers every day. The huge fuel costs incurred decided Collins against further attempts at improving the crossing times. Improvement would certainly have been possible, but in any case Collins had no American competitors at that time. The US government rewarded the performance of the shipping company by increasing its annual subsidy to $853,000. At this time three out of four of the Collins steamers had succeeded in setting new records, and the *Pacific* and *Baltic* had achieved the highest accolade of the Blue Riband; indeed, the *Baltic* held on to it until 1856 – a period of almost five years.

In spite of these successes, the Collins Line had already passed its zenith. The company's downfall was now initiated by a dreadful catastrophe. On 27 September 1854 the *Arctic* collided with the small French steamer *Vesta* in dense fog, 60 nautical miles south of Cape Race. It was feared that the French vessel would sink, so the *Arctic* stayed close by and Captain Luce lowered a boat to pick up passengers from the *Vesta* should that be required. However, the French crew managed to seal the leaks, and the *Vesta* at last took up a slow course for Newfoundland, and disappeared into the fog. It was only at this point that the crew of the *Arctic* became aware of the serious damage to their own vessel. Captain Luce now made his own attempt to reach Newfoundland, which was four hours distant. However, the water was now rising quickly and after half an hour the boiler fires were extinguished. In the meantime, a heavy sea had come up making it difficult to lower away the lifeboats. Some were dashed to pieces on the ship's sides while others drifted away. In a desperate hurry the crew lashed together a raft on which seventy-six persons embarked, but just two days later only one survivor was rescued from it. The *Arctic* sank approximately four hours after the collision. The number of people rescued was 59, while 332 drowned, among them the wife of the shipping company owner Collins, and his two children.

Collins continued to run the company, despite this tragic stroke of fate – perhaps even to prevent the accident destroying him as well. A replacement ship was ordered, but the *Adriatic*'s construction made only slow progress. On 23 January 1856 came a second blow. The *Pacific* left Liverpool with more than 180 persons on board, but the ship never arrived in New York. In desperation Collins chartered a steamer, loaded it with rescue equipment and had it search the course of the missing ship – but in vain.

Collins now came under considerable criticism, and his great successes, so widely proclaimed at the time, were all but forgotten. Since Collins had lost two of his ships, his ability to carry mail was greatly reduced, and the American postal authorities responded by reducing the subsidy to its original level, a cut of more than one half. The final blow was the considerable delay in completing the *Adriatic*, which had still not been delivered. She was not launched until the end of 1857, and by then it was too late to turn back the tide. The fate of the shipping company was sealed, and in 1858 Collins closed down his operations.

The Last Paddle Steamers

The Cunard Liners *Persia* and *Scotia*, 1856 to 1872

IN THE years after 1850 the American Collins Line had gradually collected all the records in terms of speed, size and luxury, and for the Cunard directors the challenge was to make a powerful response to these successes. The company had already reacted by initiating a direct Liverpool–New York service, and in any case the Cunard ships were neither substantially slower nor significantly less luxurious than the Collins liners. However, this first competitive skirmish between the North Atlantic steamer companies made it very clear how effective a display of superlatives could be to the general public. Speed in particular played an important role, as sea voyages were considered arduous and unpleasant, and any means of shortening the crossing was very welcome for that reason alone. It did not seem to matter that the fractions of a knot which made one ship faster than another did not result in a significantly shorter crossing–the faster ships simply offered greater appeal.

In 1854 Cunard for the first time ordered the building of a new ship with the express aim of winning back the company's lost pre-eminence in every aspect of crossing the Atlantic°. The shipyard of Robert Napier & Sons was awarded the contract for a vessel which would be the world's largest ship at that time, and would also represent the first ocean-going paddle steamer built of iron. The launch of the *Persia* on 3 July 1855 was celebrated as a great national event and on her trials on 8 January 1856 she achieved an almost incredible speed of 17 knots. She was not able to get close to this speed on her record Atlantic crossings, however, for fuel consumption would have been prohibitive. The requirement to be economical with coal was crucial, and even at

her normal speed of 13 knots the *Persia* still consumed as much as 145 tons of coal per day.

The *Persia* left harbour for her maiden voyage on 26 January 1856, three days after the final departure of the ill-fated *Pacific*, whose tragic sinking signalled the end of the American competition. Collins no longer represented a threat to the British and, indeed, Cunard was faced with no real challenger right through to the 1870s. Nonetheless, Cunard placed an order for an even faster ship in 1860. In fact, a sister ship to the *Persia* had already been planned while the first vessel was under construction, but after the collapse of Collins there had been no great urgency about the matter.

The accidents involving the *Arctic* and *Pacific* caused considerable re-thinking on the subject of maritime safety, a subject which had always had a high priority with Cunard in any case. Early in his career Samuel Cunard had stated his 'standing order' and commanded his captains to adhere to it; it related to ship, passengers and mail and he exhorted them to bring them safely over and bring them safely back. Safety was all-important. As a result of the losses at sea the already high safety standards of

°Isherwood, John H, 'Cunard Liner Persia of 1856', *Sea Breezes*, November 1966, p766

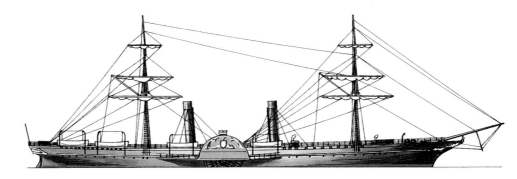

Profile of *Scotia* of 1862. The *Scotia* marked the end of the age of the paddle steamer for trans-oceanic crossings.

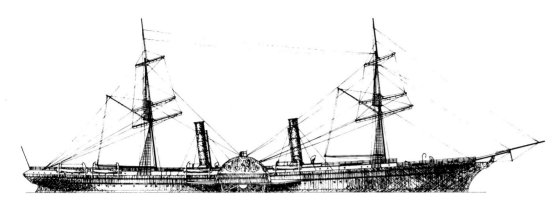

Profile of *Persia* of 1856.

The *Persia* was the first iron steamer to win the Blue Riband in 1856.

the *Persia* were revised yet again for the new ship. The vessel featured seven watertight compartments; extra reinforcements were fitted to the forward bulkhead; and this part of the ship was also fitted with buoyancy chambers—a form of double-hull. Contemporary commentators expressed considerable amazement that the decision had been made once again in favour of a paddle wheel steamer, as by this time screw propulsion was finally acknowledged as superior. However, this decision was influenced by Cunard's contractual partner—the Admiralty—which at that time still preferred paddle propulsion for its mail steamers.[°]

The ship to finally emerge was the *Scotia*, a 3781grt paddle steamer of iron construction—the world's last ocean-going

[°]Isherwood, John H, 'Cunard Liner "Scotia"', *Sea Breezes*, vol 11, 1951, p382

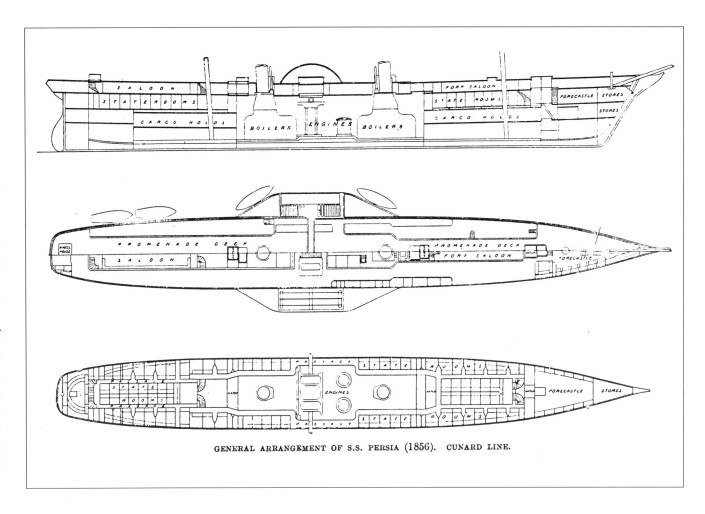

Longitudinal cross-section and deck plans of the *Persia* clearly show the way the internal space was divided up on iron-built Atlantic paddle steamers.

GENERAL ARRANGEMENT OF S.S. PERSIA (1856). CUNARD LINE.

paddle steamer. She was not the world's largest ship, however, as the *Great Eastern* had held that distinction since her launch in 1858, but in every other characteristic the *Scotia* ranked as the world's number one. It was not until December 1863, two years after her launch, that she took the Blue Riband from the *Persia*, her sister ship, but she made up for this by improving the speed by a full 1.35 knots.

The *Persia* and *Scotia* were the last paddle steamers built for international service. The *Persia* was retired after twelve years of service in 1868, but *Scotia* remained in the passenger service of the Cunard Line until 1876, by which time she was certainly an anachronism. She had been obliged to relinquish the Blue Riband in 1872, this time to a screw-driven steamer, and it was to be thirteen years before Cunard was able to win it back again.

---

ss *Persia*

Owner: Cunard Line, Liverpool.

Builder: Robert Napier & Sons, Glasgow.

Specification: 3300grt / 1200dwt / 398ft overall length / 45ft beam / one two-cylinder side lever steam engine; Napier / 3600ihp / two side paddle wheels / 13 knots / 200 first-class, 50 second-class passengers.

Career: 3.7.1855 launched / 8.1.1856 trials. Largest ship in the world at that time /

26.1.1856 maiden voyage Liverpool–New York / 19. to 29.4.1856 won Blue Riband at 13.11 knots, later improved several times / 5.1856 first record crossing in easterly direction / 1868 laid up in Birkenhead. Engines removed / 1868 to MacArthur & Wilson, Glasgow. Planned refit as sailing ship, not implemented / 1872 towed to London, broken up.

ss *Scotia*

Owner: Cunard Line, Liverpool.

Builder: Robert Napier & Sons, Glasgow.

Specification: 3871grt / 1400dwt / 400ft overall length / 47.8ft beam / one two-cylinder side lever steam engine; Napier / 4000ihp / two side paddle wheels / 13.5 knots / 273 first-class, 50 second-class passengers (or 250 troops if required).

Career: 25.6.1861 launched / 3.1862 trials /

10.5.1862 maiden voyage Liverpool–Queens-town–New York / 19. to 27.7.1863 won Blue Riband at 14.46 knots / 12.1863 record crossing in easterly direction / 5.1876 laid up / 1879 refit at Laird, Birkenhead as cable-layer, commissioned by Telegraph Construction & Maintenance Company. 4667grt, twin-screw propulsion, 11.5 knots / 1902 to Commercial Pacific Cable Company / 11.3.1904 stranded off Guam.

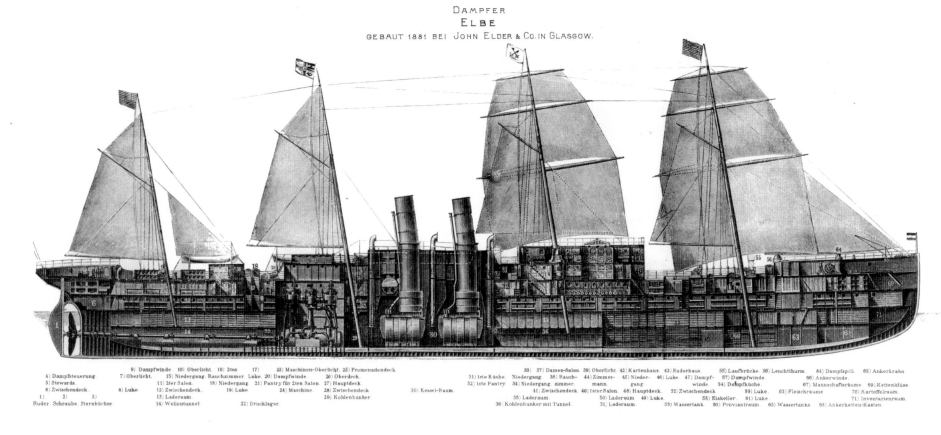

DAMPFER
ELBE
GEBAUT 1881 BEI JOHN ELDER & CO. IN GLASGOW.

			9) Dampfwinde. 10) Oberlicht. 16) 2tes	17)	23) Maschinen-Oberlicht. 25) Promenadendeck.		33) 37) Damen-Salon. 39) Oberlicht. 42) Kartenhaus. 43) Ruderhaus.		55) Laufbrücke. 56) Leuchtthurm	64) Dampfspill. 65) Ankerkrahn.
4) Dampfsteuerung.	7) Oberlicht.	15) Niedergang. Rauchzimmer. Luke. 20) Dampfwinde.	26) Oberdeck.	31) 1ste Küche. Niedergang. 38) Rauch- 44) Zimmer- 45) Nieder- 46) Luke. 47) Dampf- 57) Dampfwinde.	66) Ankerwinde.
5) Stewards.		11) 2ter Salon. 18) Niedergang. 21) Pantry für 2ten Salon. 27) Hauptdeck.		32) 1ste Pantry. 34) Niedergang. mann gang. winde. 54) Dampfküche.	67) Mannschaftsräume. 69) Kettenklüse.
6) Zwischendeck.	8) Luke.	12) Zwischendeck. 19) Luke. 24) Maschine. 28) Zwischendeck	30) Kessel-Raum.	41) Zwischendeck 40) 1ster Salon. 48) Hauptdeck. 52) Zwischendeck	59) Luke. 62) Fleischräume. 70) Kartoffelraum.
1) 2) 3)		13) Laderaum.		35) Laderaum. 50) Laderaum 49) Luke. 53) Eiskeller. 61) Luke.	71) Inventarienraum.
Ruder. Schraube. Sternbüchse.		14) Wellentunnel 22) Drucklager.		36) Kohlenbunker mit Tunnel 51) Laderaum. 53) Wassertank. 60) Proviantraum. 63) Wassertanks.	68) Ankerketten-Kasten.

This longitudinal cross-section of the *Elbe* gives a clear illustration of the technology and space utilisation of the express steamers around 1880.

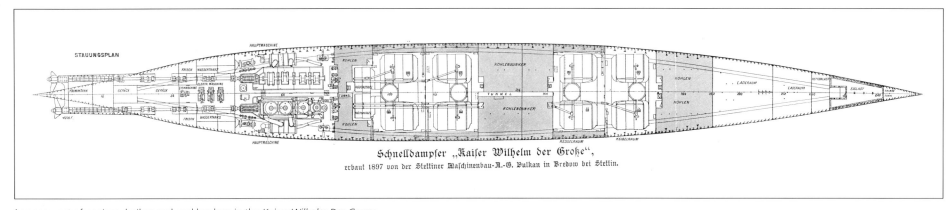

STAUUNGSPLAN

Schnelldampfer „Kaiser Wilhelm der Große",
erbaut 1897 von der Stettiner Maschinenbau-A.-G. Vulkan in Bredow bei Stettin.

Arrangement of engines, boilers and coal bunkers in the *Kaiser Wilhelm Der Grosse*.

50

The Second Era: 1872 to 1907

Screw Steamers with Steam Piston Engines

The Propulsion Technology of the Express Screw Steam Ships

IN ITS earliest form the ship's propeller is as old as steam navigation itself, but it was not until the 1830s that screws of adequate efficiency were developed. A famous comparative trial was organised by the British Admiralty in 1845, pitting the *Alecto* paddle steamer against the *Rattler*, a screw steamer, and in every respect the outcome was a convincing victory for the screw ship. In the same year Isambard Kingdom Brunel's steamer *Great Britain* was introduced into the North Atlantic service, and this ship also proved excellent in every technical respect, though she was not a fast vessel. However, a screw-propelled steam ship did not engage in the contest for the Blue Riband until 1872.

In fact, it was impossible to produce a significant improvement in the performance during the first Blue Riband era without finding a method of increasing steam pressure. In the 1860s engineers finally developed boilers which could operate at a pressure of 4at, and this higher pressure was the key to economic operation of compound engines (also known as composite or double-expansion steam engines), in which the steam was allowed to expand twice. The compound engine is equipped with two cylinders of different diameter. The steam first enters the smaller one at a pressure of 4at, but the pressure of the exhaust steam (2at) is still great enough to perform useful work in the second, larger cylinder. This technology produced a fuel saving of 33 per cent compared with the earlier engines. It was the development of this new technology which made it possible for the White Star Line liner, the *Adriatic*, to compete in the Blue Riband contest in 1872 and win.

Two of the four engines of the Lloyd steamer *Kaiser Wilhelm II*, arranged in tandem pairs, which was the largest reciprocating steam engine system ever installed in a ship. Total power output was 44,500ihp, and each of the two pairs of engines acted on one propeller shaft. The raised sections, looking like towers, housed the high-pressure cylinders, with the first intermediate-pressure cylinders below them. Steam from these cylinders was passed into the second intermediate-pressure cylinder and finally to the low-pressure cylinder.

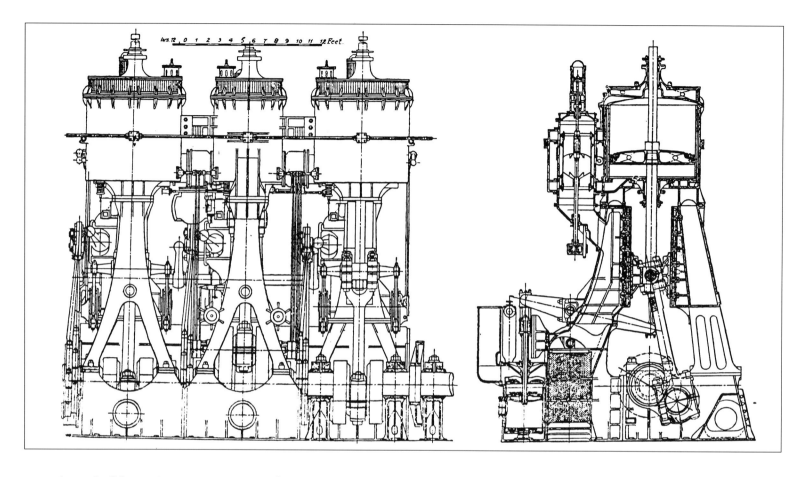

At the end of the 1870s steam pressures of 7at were achieved, and this in turn made it possible to expand the compound engine again by adding a second low-pressure cylinder. Around 1880 the Guion liners were the first steam ships to reach a speed of 16 knots, and the new engines were the key to this. By the early 1890s new cylindrical boilers could produce a steam pressure of 12at, and this allowed the breakthrough to be made in the development of the triple-expansion engine – a logical extension of the compound engine – in which the steam passes through the high-pressure, intermediate-pressure and low-pressure cylinders in turn. This type of engine could also be constructed with four cylinders by configuring the low-pressure cylinder as a double unit, and if the high-pressure cylinder were also doubled, the number of cylinders could rise to five. Triple-expansion engines

consumed up to 30 per cent less coal than conventional compound engines.

In 1900 the Hapag vessel *Deutschland* won the Blue Riband, the first steam ship powered by a quadruple-expansion engine to do so. This type of engine required a steam pressure of 15at, and the sequence of cylinders was high-pressure, intermediate-pressure twice – with different piston diameters – and finally low-pressure. This development represented the final stage of refinement of the steam piston engine. The 46,000ihp produced by the quadruple expansion engines of the Lloyd steamers *Kaiser Wilhelm II* and *Kronprinzessin Cecilie* made them the most powerful reciprocating engines ever installed in a ship; a further increase in power no longer made sense in terms of economics.

Technology versus Subsidy

The White Star Line, 1872 to 1882

♦♦♦

THE FACT that so many contestants for the Blue Riband suddenly appeared on the North Atlantic route is due to developments both in economics and technology. Although Cunard and Collins had kept the competition in fast steamer travel to themselves for a period of almost twenty years, this was by no means due to a lack of interest on the part of others. In the 1860s all the major seafaring nations had established their own transatlantic services, and Great Britain could boast a large number of shipping companies in addition to Cunard. Many of these enterprises would have been only too glad to commission high-speed steam ships so that they could compete on level terms with the big companies like Collins and Cunard. However, the crux of the matter was the state subsidy; these smaller companies received no subsidies, and with the state of technology at the time no fast service could be operated economically without state assistance.

Around 1870 the situation changed. British engineers succeeded in refining the design of the compound engine to the

Profile of *Adriatic* of 1872.

Profile of *Britannic* (above) and of *Germanic* (below) of 1874/75.

point where it was ready for widespread sale, and these engines were around 100 per cent more efficient than earlier power plants. Since these engines were so economical in terms of coal consumption, new perspectives opened up for non-subsidised shipping companies; for the first time they could reasonably consider building fast steamers. The risk had become a calculable one, and decisive entrepreneurs soon detected and filled the new gap in the market.

Thomas Ismay was undoubtedly the most successful of these newcomers. For many years he gained experience as Director of the National Line, then in 1869 he founded the Oceanic Steam Navigation Company in Liverpool, which became popularly known as the White Star Line. He ordered his first six ships from his Belfast-based friend Edward J Harland, of the Harland & Wolff company, and these vessels were launched between 1871 and 1872. They were the first fast ships with compound steam engines, but they also incorporated other revolutionary innovations. They were the first passenger ships to feature a boat deck on the midship superstructure; and whereas first-class passengers had been accommodated in the aftership on earlier liners, here they were housed in the middle of the ship, where the rolling and pitching movements were least disturbing. All the

ss *Adriatic*

Owner: White Star Line, Liverpool.

Builder: Harland & Wolff, Belfast; Yard No. 77.

Specification: 3868grt / 454ft overall length / 41ft beam / one four-cylinder tandem compound steam engine; Maudslay, Sons & Field / 3000ihp / one screw / 14 knots / 166 first-class, 1000 third-class passengers.

Career: 17.10.1871 launched / 11.4.1872 maiden voyage Liverpool–Queenstown–New York / 5.1872 won Blue Riband at 14.53 knots / 1884 second-class passengers admitted / 12.1897 de-commissioned / 1899 broken up in Preston.

ss *Britannic*

Owner: White Star Line, Liverpool.

Builder: Harland & Wolff, Belfast; Yard No. 83.

Specification: 5004grt / 468ft overall length / 45ft beam / one four-cylinder tandem compound steam engine; Maudslay, Sons & Field / 5000ihp / one screw / 15 knots / 220 first-class, 1500 third-class passengers.

Career: Laid down as *Hellenic* / 3.2.1874 launched / 25.6.1874 maiden voyage Liverpool–Queenstown–New York / 11.1876 won Blue Riband at 15.43 knots / 1899 transport vessel in Boer War. Broken up in Hamburg 1903.

ss *Germanic*

Owner: White Star Line, Liverpool.

Builder: Harland & Wolff, Belfast; Yard No. 85.

Specification: 5008grt / 470ft overall length / 45ft beam / one four-cylinder tandem compound steam engine; Maudslay, Sons & Field / 5000ihp / one screw / 15 knots / 220 first-class, 1500 third-class passengers.

Career: 15.7.1874 launched / 20.5.1875 maiden voyage Liverpool–Queenstown–New York / 30.7 to 7.8.1875 won Blue Riband at 14.65 knots / 4.1876 improved to 15.76 knots / 2.1876 record crossing in easterly direction / 1895 refit, extra deck, longer funnels, 5066grt / 13.2.1899 capsized in New

York when loading coal / 7.6.1899 salvaged, repaired in Belfast, re-commissioned / 10.1903 laid up / 1904 four charter voyages Southampton–New York for the American Line / 1905 renamed *Ottawa*, with Dominion Line, Liverpool. First-class now second-class / 27.4.1905 to 2.9.1909 Liverpool–Montreal service / 15.3.1911 to Constantinople, renamed *Gul Djemal*, for Denizbank Denizyollari Idaresi, Constantinople. Service in Black Sea / 3.5.1915 torpedoed in Marmara Sea by British submarine *E14* / raised / 6.10.1920 first voyage Constantinople–New York / 11.1921 laid up / 1928 renamed *Gulcemal* / 16.11.1950 to Messina for breaking up.

The first White Star steamers were the first liners with the saloon located amidships, and with the superstructure projecting markedly higher than the main deck, as shown in this photograph of the *Adriatic*.

cabins were on the outer sides of the ship, and had running hot water. These liners were also the first fast steamers with steer-age accommodation for emigrants. The latter were not even obliged to sleep in large dormitories – as in the vessels of other shipping companies – but had simple four-berth cabins, with access to a roomy saloon. In short, they revolutionised passenger comfort on the rough Atlantic seas. All the White Star ships, including all later vessels, were built

Thomas Henry Ismay (1837-1899), one of the most progressive and inventive ship owners on the North Atlantic route.

The *Germanic* in her early years of service, still carrying two masts with yards, and low funnels. This steam ship had a highly varied life, and was not scrapped until 1950.

Edward James Harland (1831-1895), co-founder of the famed Belfast shipyard of Harland & Wolff; he it was that converted Ismay's brilliant ideas into equally brilliant ships.

The White Star liner *Britannic* in Liverpool with her longer funnels, extended in 1890.

John Elder (1824-1869), who brought the compound steam engine to technical maturity.

in the renowned Harland & Wolff yards. A characteristic feature of the White Star express steamers of the nineteenth century was the high ratio of length to beam of 10:1. In accordance with the old shipbuilding principle of 'length equals speed', this layout guaranteed high speed combined with low fuel consumption. The last two ships of this series of six were the 3900grt *Adriatic* and *Celtic*. In May 1872 the *Adriatic* finally earned the Blue Riband with a crossing speed of 14.5 knots, which she subsequently relinquished to another White Star liner, the *Germanic*, in 1875.

The sister ships *Britannic* and *Germanic* represented further developments of the first ships already described. They were the work of Edward J Harland himself, and he incorporated many improvements in the vessels based on the experience gained with the first ships. Although the first White Star ships had been of outstanding quality, these two new vessels, launched in 1874

and 1875 respectively, pushed all the liners belonging to rival shipping companies into the second division. They were the company's top ships for fifteen years, which is a quite astonishing length of time in that era of rapid technical progress. Even their coal consumption of only around 95 tons per day at 16 knots was outstandingly low. The *Britannic* was initially fitted with an adjustable-height propeller shaft which could be lowered when the vessel reached deep water, with the purpose of achieving better efficiency. It is not clear whether this innovation gave any advantage at all, but it certainly had one obvious drawback: serious vibration forced the idea to be abandoned after nine voyages, and the ship was converted to a normal stern with a fixed shaft. The *Britannic* won the Blue Riband in 1876, and the *Germanic* won it twice, in 1875 and 1876. In so doing these ships raised their average speed for the Atlantic crossing from 14.53 to 15.76 knots.

THE INMAN LINE, 1875 TO 1876

The Inman Line was founded as far back as 1850 under the name Liverpool & Philadelphia Steam Ship Company, but in 1857 the firm adopted the new name of the Liverpool, New York & Philadelphia Steam Ship Company. In 1875 its name changed again to the Inman Steamship Company, until finally, in 1886, it assumed the name of Inman & International Steamship Company. The firm began building express liners in 1869; it was the first non-subsidised line to do so, before, even, the White Star Line. In December 1869 the 3081grt *City of Brussels* improved the record for the easterly crossing to 14.74 knots, and other Inman ships just failed to produce records on their voyages in both directions.

When the plans of the White Star Line to build the *Britannic* and *Germanic* came to the attention of the Inman board, the directors decided to commission the building of a ship which would be at least the equal of the new ships of the rival company, and every effort would be made to surpass them. The contract was granted to the renowned yard of Caird & Co. in the Scottish town of Greenock. Inman had built what were termed 'long ships' before even the White Star Line had done so, and the new steamers were to be built with a length to beam ratio of no less than 11:1. This figure was unprecedented, and was never attempted again. Incidentally, although fears were expressed that the liner would roll excessively due to its slender hull, they turned out to be unfounded.

The *City of Berlin* held the Blue Riband for one year before she had to relinquish it to the White Star Line again in 1876. The photograph shows the liner after a major refit in 1887.

On trials the new *City of Berlin* gave a disappointing account of herself. She achieved a speed of only 14.82 knots over the one-mile course, which was less than the required service speed of 15 knots. The company also considered the fuel consumption to be excessive. However, it is evident that some machinery improvements were carried out before the ship was commissioned.

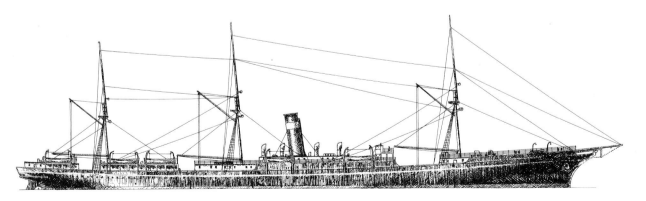

Profile of *City of Berlin* of 1875.

William Inman (1825-1881) kept faith with the conventional clipper stem on his modern express steamers.

The success of the Guion liners *Arizona* and *Oregon* inspired the Liverpool National Line to build new steamers. Its 5,528grt *America* was built by J & G Thomson in Glasgow and delivered in 1884. She achieved respectable speeds. In June 1884 she completed a crossing in the easterly direction which took less time than the record holder *Oregon*, but without exceeding her overall speed. Thus *America* never set a new record, a fate she shared with the equally unlucky *City of Rome*; in 1886 both ships shared a common schedule. Just one year later the disappointed National Line sold its express steamer to the Italian Navy.

ss *City of Brussels*

Owner: Inman Line, Liverpool.

Builder: Tod & McGregor, Glasgow.

Specification: 3081grt / 390ft reg. length / 40ft beam / one low-pressure steam engine / 3200ihp / one screw / 14 knots / 200 first-class, 600 steerage passengers.

Career: 10.8.1869 launched / 14.10.1869 maiden voyage Liverpool–Queenstown–New York / 12.1869 record crossing New York–Queenstown / 12.1871 to 5.1872 promenade deck installed, now 1000 steerage passengers, 3747grt / 1876 four-cylinder compound engine fitted / 7.1.1883 sunk in Mersey after collision with steamer *Kirby Hall*; ten dead.

ss *City of Berlin*

Owner: Inman Line, Liverpool.

Builder: Caird & Co. Greenock.

Specification: 5491grt / 520ft overall length / 44ft beam / one two-cylinder compound steam engine; Caird / 4800ihp / one screw / 15 knots / 170 first-class, 100 second-class, 1500 steerage passengers.

Career: 27.10.1874 launched / 29.4.1875 maiden voyage Liverpool–Queenstown–New York / 17. to 25.9.1875 won Blue Riband at 15.21 knots / 9.1875 record crossing in easterly direction / 1879 was first steamer to be fitted with electric internal lighting / 1887 at Laird in Birkenhead one triple-expansion engine and new boilers fitted, 6000ihp. Passenger appointments also improved / 18.3.1893 first voyage Southampton–New York / Between 1895 and 1898 seven Antwerp–New York crossings under charter to Red Star Line / 1898 renamed *Meade*, US troop transport to Philippines / 31.1.1906 burned out in San Francisco; three dead, several missing. Laid up / 1918 to US Shipping Board, Boston, as training ship / 1921 broken up in Philadelphia.

On 29 April 1875 the *City of Berlin* steamed out on her maiden voyage. With her 5491 gross tons she exceeded the size of the White Star liners, and in September she was successful in relieving the *Germanic* of the Blue Riband with an improvement of 0.6 knots. At 15.21 knots the *City of Berlin* was the first ship to exceed 15 knots when winning the Blue Riband. A year later the *Britannic* brought the Blue Riband back to the White Star Line, but that did not detract from the Inman Line's achievement in register-

ing for the first time in the list of holders of the Blue Riband. In 1879 the *City of Berlin* hit the headlines again; she was the first ship to be equipped with electric lighting– four lamps illuminated the first-class saloon, and a further two in the steerage accommodation.

THE GUION LINE, 1882 TO 1884

In 1866 the Liverpool & Great Western Steamship Company was registered, a company which was more commonly known as the Guion Line after its founder, the American-born Stephen Barker Guion. The company made itself a fine reputation in the Liverpool–New York passenger service and earned substantial profits with its emigrant ships.

By 1872 Stephen Guion had already attempted to set new speed records for the Atlantic crossing with his steam ships *Montana* and *Dakota*. With three-cylinder compound engines and oversized boilers operating at a pressure of 6.9at, the ships were capable of a top speed of 17 knots, comfortably faster than the Blue Riband record of 14.5 knots. However, the attempt did not go as planned as continual engine breakdowns and boiler problems put an end to the venture before any record was set. New boilers had to be installed and the power reduced, with the result that the steamers could only achieve 11 knots in their final form. Although two more ships of this type had been ordered, Guion very quickly cancelled them.

Even so, his ambition to create a fleet of record-breaking ships was not diminished, and in 1878 he granted a contract to John

Stephen Barker Guion (1819-1885) gained experience by working for Cunard and the National Line before founding his own shipping company in 1866.

The *Alaska*, pictured here in front of the silhouette of her home port, Liverpool, won the Blue Riband in 1882 and was also successful in the opposite direction.

Elder & Co of Glasgow for the 5147grt *Arizona*, whose technical design features, at least, seemed to offer guaranteed success. However, the ship never did manage to wrest the Blue Riband from its holder, and her sole record was a crossing in the easterly direction at just on 16 knots.

The ship, however, did achieve one record of a different kind when, on 7 November 1879, on her return voyage to Liverpool, she rammed her bow squarely into an iceberg when steaming at 16 knots. Her foreship crumpled up like a concertina, reducing her length by some 28 feet. Fortunately, the collision bulkhead did not fail, and the ship was able to reach St John's, where all the passengers disembarked safely. A temporary bow repair was carried out, after which *Arizona* steamed from St John's to Liverpool in less than seven days. The manner in which the ship survived this adventure was publicised skilfully, and the effect of the propaganda was to impress upon the press and the public

ss *Arizona*	ss *Alaska*	ss *Oregon*	

Owner: Guion Line, Liverpool.

Builder: John Elder & Co, Glasgow.

Specification: 5147grt / 2600dwt / 475ft overall length / 45ft beam / one three-cylinder compound steam engine; Elder / 6500ihp / one screw / 15 knots / 140 first-class, 70 second-class, 140 third-class, 1000 steerage passengers.

Career: 10.3.1879 launched / 31.5.1879 maiden voyage Liverpool–Queenstown–New York / 7.1879 record crossing in easterly direction / 1894 laid up in Gareloch / 1897 to William Pierce, Liverpool, for refit. Triple-expansion engine, single large funnel, 40 first-class, 1000 steerage passengers / 1898 first voyage Vancouver–Tacoma–Hong Kong–Yokohama / 1898 renamed *Hancock*, US Navy transport ship / 1903 barrack ship, Brooklyn Navy Yard / 1914 US troop transport vessel / 1918 laid up in Philadelphia / 1926 broken up.

Owner: Guion Line, Liverpool.

Builder: John Elder & Co, Glasgow.

Specification: 6932grt / 520ft overall length / 50ft beam / one three-cylinder compound steam engine; Elder / 8300ihp / one screw / 16 knots / 350 first-class, 1000 steerage passengers.

Career: 15.7.1881 launched / 30.10.1881 maiden voyage Liverpool–Queenstown–New York / 9. to 16.4.1882 won Blue Riband with 16.07 knots / 6.1882 record crossing in easterly direction / Both records improved by 1884 / 5.1894 laid up in Gareloch / 1897 renamed *Magallanes* for charter, operated by the Cia. Transatlantica Espanola as troop transport ship in Spanish-American war / 1898 laid up in Clyde / 1899 sold for breaking up, then sold again. Accommodation ship in Barrow / 1902 broken up in Preston.

Owner: Guion Line, Liverpool.

Builder: John Elder & Co, Glasgow.

Specification: 7375grt / 2400dwt / 521ft overall length / 54ft beam / one three-cylinder compound steam engine; Elder / 12,500ihp / one screw / 17.5 knots / 340 first-class, 92 second-class, 110 third-class, 1000 steerage passengers.

Career: 23.6.1883 launched / 6.10.1883 maiden voyage Liverpool–Queenstown–New York / 4.1884 record crossing in easterly direction / 13. to 19.4.1884 won Blue Riband at 18.56 knots / 5.1884 to Cunard Line, Liverpool / 7.6.1884 Cunard voyage Liverpool–Queenstown–New York / Records repeatedly improved until 1885/1885 auxiliary cruiser in Royal Navy / 14.11.1885 returned to Liverpool–Queenstown–New York service / 14.3.1886 collided with schooner *Charles Morse* 18 nautical miles East of Long Island; schooner sank with all

hands. The *Oregon* also sank slowly. 900 persons – passengers and crew – took to the boats and were then rescued by the North German Lloyd ship *Fulda*.

that this was a particularly safe ship. Captain Herbert Brooks and his First Officer did not fare so well; both were banned from seafaring for six months.

Guion's next attempt brought the success for which he had yearned. The *Alaska*, built by the Elder yard and of almost 7000grt, came into service in 1881, and in the following year broke all the speed records. By 1884 she had improved the record speeds repeatedly. These successes were a huge encouragement to Guion, and he subsequently ordered from Elder the slightly larger *Oregon*, whose service speed was expected to exceed that of *Alaska* by two knots. In October 1883 *Oregon* was commissioned, but during that winter she did not undertake any record attempts; instead the engineers carefully ran-in her engines. In the spring of 1884 she was then able to try for the records, and as expected relieved her predecessor of the Blue Riband and the record for the easterly passage. For the first time the mark for the Blue Riband had broken 18 knots, the record now standing at precisely 18.56 knots.

At this point, just when Guion had finally achieved his ambition after more than ten years of effort, the fates were to relieve him of the fruits of his success. Certainly he contributed to his own downfall in building the *Oregon* which so stretched the company financially. After just a few months, in which the ship had been able to secure the greatest of all triumphs for him, he was obliged to sell his flagship in order to settle Elder's bills. To whom did he sell her? To none other than Cunard, of all firms.

In view of the eventual turn of events, it is intriguing to wonder what might have been going on behind the scenes. On the one hand there was the ambitious Mr Guion, whose highly innovative technical demands had greatly enhanced the reputation of the Elder yard (and of his successor firm Fairfield), and made it for many years the first port of call for anyone wanting a fast steam ship. Then there was the Elder yard, which had granted the most generous of settlement terms to Guion,

but had then dropped him at the first sign of financial difficulties. And last, in the background, was the Cunard Line, which in the meantime had ordered two express steamers of the *Oregon* type. One cannot but help imagining that Cunard, at the first sign of Guion's weakness, might have given a discreet nod in the direction of Elder, and the yard then immediately and obediently refused Guion credit. Whatever the background, the net result was that in one swoop Cunard was relieved of his most serious rival, and also procured his best ship at a low price – complete with the Blue Riband. Naturally, the price would have been low, as there was no other potential purchaser for such a ship at that time. The Elder may have reasonably hoped to obtain the goodwill of the Cunard company for having instigated the turn of events, Cunard was a company which – thanks to its subsidy income – could become a very important client. Indeed, only a few years later the yard was granted a contract for the construction of two top-quality express liners.

Guion soldiered on with the remainder of his fleet, doing badly more often than not, until eventually his shipping company went into liquidation in 1894, brought about by the ever increasing competition on the North Atlantic.

Guion's first ship, the *Arizona*, failed to fulfil the high expectations made for her; the best she could achieve was one record in the easterly direction in 1879.

The *Oregon* exceeded the performance of the *Alaska* by 1.5 knots. In 1884 Guion sold her to the Cunard Line, together with the Blue Riband – a unique instance.

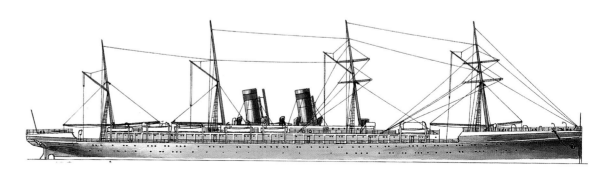

Profile of the Guion liner *Alaska* of 1881.

Profile of the *Oregon* of 1883.

The German Fast Steam Ships of the Fluesse Class

❖❖❖

THIS SHORT chapter, and another starting on page 74, deal with two ship classes which took part in the competition for the Blue Riband, albeit unsuccessfully, and in so doing presaged a significant international development. As already mentioned, holding the Blue Riband did not necessarily mean that the shipping company concerned was necessarily the premier one on the North Atlantic, as witness the ships of White Star Line. The record-breaking ship was not necessarily a superlative vessel in every respect.

When analysing the performance of German ships in the contest for the fastest Atlantic crossing it is important to remember that, compared with all the British and French ships, the

The North German Lloyd steamer *Eider* of 1884.

63

The boat deck of the first German express steamer *Elbe* of 1881.

Germans were handicapped by a sea voyage 450 to 500 nautical miles longer. This additional stretch – from Bremerhaven to Southampton or Cherbourg – extended the total distance to be covered to approximately 3700 nautical miles, about 15 per cent longer. For the 16-knot steamers of the *Fluesse* (Rivers) class this meant one extra day's overall journey time. Naturally, the ships' design had to allow for the additional weight and volume of coal and victuals required for the extra time at sea.

Not one of the eleven *Fluesse* class steamers mentioned here was ever able to win the Blue Riband, although the Norddeutscher Lloyd (North German Lloyd) company initially had aspirations in that direction, inspired by the fast Guion ships described in the previous chapter. Between 1881 and 1891 North German Lloyd commissioned a total of eleven steamers of this class, all of them named after German rivers. Apart from the last two ships, *Spree* and *Havel*, which were built in 1890 in Stettin, all the ships were built at the Elder yard in Glasgow, and its successor, Fairfield.

This armada of ships meant that the Lloyd possessed the largest fleet of fast steamers of all the world's shipping companies. The ships were employed on the Bremerhaven–Southampton–New York route, known as the Channel route, whereas the British shipping companies ran from Liverpool via Cobh (then Queenstown) to New York. The table on this page provides an interesting comparison between the top international express steamers which were operating in the period 1874 to 1891. The Lloyd steamers were always one step behind the competitors in terms of size, speed and passenger capacity, partly because the lock gates to the Bremerhaven Kaiserhafen (the Emperor harbour) limited the ships' size and subsequent performance.

However, there were three areas in which these ships were highly significant. First, during the 1880s they made North German Lloyd the leading international passenger carrier. No shipping company carried more passengers to New York and the company maintained this position until 1912. Second, the fixtures and fittings of these steamers were so luxurious and comfortable that they were acknowledged internationally as the first true luxury liners°.

The steamers of the Rivers Class (printed bold) and their contemporaries

Name	Shipping company	First voyage	grt	kn°	Passengers 1st	2nd	Steerage
BRITANNIC	White Star	25. June 1874	5004	15	220	–	1500
CITY OF BERLIN	Inman	9. Apr. 1875	5491	15	170	100	1500
GERMANIC	White Star	20. May 1875	5008	15	220	–	1500
ARIZONA	Guion	31. May 1879	5147	15	140	70	1140
ELBE	Nd. Lloyd	26. June 1881	4510	15	179	142	796
ALASKA	Guion	31. Oct. 1881	6932	16	350	–	1000
WERRA	Nd. Lloyd	12. Oct. 1882	4817	16	190	144	868
FULDA	Nd. Lloyd	14. Mar 1883	4816	16	190	146	865
NORMANDIE	C.G.T.	5. May 1883	6283	16	205	76	1000
EIDER	Nd. Lloyd	19. Mar 1884	5129	16	194	134	876
EMS	Nd. Lloyd	4. June 1884	5129	16	194	135	876
AMERICA	National	28. May 1884	5528	17	300	–	700
OREGON	Guion	7. June 1884	7374	18	340	92	1110
UMBRIA	Cunard	1. Nov 1884	7718	19	550	–	800
ALLER	Nd. Lloyd	24. Apr 1886	4964	17	224	90	660
LA CHAMPAGNE	C.G.T.	22. May 1886	7087	17	390	65	600
TRAVE	Nd. Lloyd	5. June 1886	4996	17	224	90	660
LA BOURGOGNE	C.G.T.	19. June 1886	7395	17	390	65	600
LA BRETAGNE	C.G.T.	14. Aug 1886	7112	17	390	65	600
SAALE	Nd. Lloyd	18. Aug 1886	4965	17	224	90	660
LA GASCOGNE	C.G.T.	18. Sept 1886	7395	17	390	65	600
LAHN	Nd. Lloyd	1. Feb 1888	5661	18	224	104	600
CITY OF NEW YORK	Inman	1. Aug 1888	10499	20	540	200	1000
CITY OF PARIS	Inman	3. Apr 1889	10449	20	540	200	1000
AUGUSTA VICTORIA	Hapag	10. May 1889	7661	18	400	120	580
COLUMBIA	Hapag	18. Jul 1889	7578	18	400	120	580
TEUTONIC	White Star	7. Aug 1889	9984	19	300	190	1000
MAJESTIC	White Star	2. Apr 1890	9965	19	300	190	1000
NORMANNIA	Hapag	22. May 1890	8716	19	420	172	700
SPREE	Nd. Lloyd	10. Nov 1890	6963	18,5	274	148	384
HAVEL	Nd. Lloyd	5. Feb 1891	6963	18,5	274	148	384
FÜRST BISMARCK	Hapag	8. May 1891	8874	19	420	172	700

°Service speed in knots

The French C.G.T. ships and Hapag ships from Hamburg were direct competitors to North German Lloyd on the Channel route, whereas the British steamers ran from Liverpool to New York.

° Brinnin, John Malcolm, and Ganlin, Kenneth, *Grand Luxe: The Transatlantic Style* (New York 1988).

Title page of a cabin plan of the *Fulda* of 1882.

Third, in the statistics of the US American Postmaster these steamers held the leading places for the fastest mail route from New York to London for a period of many years. The Postmaster's calculations included the total duration of the mail run from New York to London, and, as the train journey from Liverpool was longer than that from Southampton, the German ships had a small advantage.

So here was a shipping company which was by no means dependent upon winning the Blue Riband although it had hoped to do so. It offered luxury and comfort, rather than the ultimate in speed. The company also proved that subsidies were not an absolute necessity, for North German Lloyd generated this business entirely by its own efforts, without state support.

This was the style of internal appointments designed by the Bremen architect Johannes G. Poppe, which earned North German Lloyd its reputation of having invented luxury at sea. Here is the *Lahn*'s first-class dining room with the gallery of the ladies' saloon, and above that the light shaft and glazed cupola.

The Last of the Single-Screw Express Steamers
The Cunard Line, 1885 to 1889

◆◆◆

IN 1884 the Cunard Line would have regained the Blue Riband even had the company not purchased the *Oregon*. In 1883 Cunard had ordered the two sister ships *Umbria* and *Etruria* from John Elder & Co, and these were the first Blue Riband contestants to be built of steel. Steel was a new material for shipbuilding, and at this time was just beginning to supersede the more brittle iron. The greater strength of steel permitted greater dimensions in shipbuilding, and this was very soon evident from the rapid growth in the size of ships. Although they had steel hulls, in other respects the two new Cunarders were rather orthodox vessels. They were equipped with compound engines, which by this time were considered merely conventional, and their immense power of 14,500ihp was transmitted to a single screw shaft. The *Umbria* came into service in November

The *Umbria* in 1890 at her home port of Liverpool.

Profiles of the Cunard fast steamer *Umbria* above, and *Etruria*, below, of 1884/85.

ss *Umbria*

Owner: Cunard Line, Liverpool.

Builder: John Elder & Co, Glasgow.

Specification: 7718grt / 519ft overall length / 57ft beam / two three-cylinder compound engines; Elder / 14,500ihp / one screw / 19 knots / 550 first-class, 160 second-class, 800 third-class passengers.

Career: 26.6.1884 launched / 1.11.1884 maiden voyage Liverpool–Queenstown–New York / 27.5 to 2.6.1887 won Blue Riband at 19.22 knots / 1890 8128grt / 31.12.1892 to 1.4.1893 shaft failure and repair / 1.1900 transport ship in Boer War, two voyages / 21.7.1900 again Liverpool–Queenstown–New York / 1910 broken up.

ss *Etruria*

Owner: Cunard Line, Liverpool.

Builder: John Elder & Co, Glasgow.

Specification: 7718grt / 519ft overall length / 57ft beam / two three-cylinder compound engines; Elder / 14,500ihp / one screw / 19 knots / 550 first-class, 160 second-class, 800 third-class passengers.

Career: 20.9.1884 launched / 25.4.1885 maiden voyage Liverpool–Queenstown–New York / 8.1885 record crossing in easterly direction / 16. to 22.8.1885 won Blue Riband at 18.73 knots / improved both records in 1888 / 1890 8120grt / 1902 out of service for several months due to shaft failure / 9.1909 laid up / 11.1909 to Preston, broken up.

The *Umbria* encounters *Etruria* on the open seas, as seen by a contemporary illustrator.

1884, and the *Etruria* followed in April 1885. Both ships pushed the record mark for the Blue Riband up to more than 19 knots, and the *Etruria* also took the record as fastest ship in the easterly direction. These records stood until 1889, when the era of the twin-screw ships began.

Incidentally, both ships fell victim to that characteristic accident of the single-screw express steamer, and one which their captains feared above all. This was a fracture of the propeller shaft due to the stress of running constantly at maximum load, and it was a failure which was by no means an uncommon occurrence. The *Umbria* suffered this fate in December 1892, and was towed in to New York on New Year's Day. After temporary repairs had been carried out, the ship undertook the home voyage without passengers, and then entered the dockyard for permanent repair in late March. In 1902 the *Etruria* suffered an even worse fate, when its propeller was lost in mid-Atlantic, taking the rudder and rudderpost with it. Bereft of power and steering, the ship drifted in the Atlantic for days, at the mercy of wind and weather. Radio had not yet been invented, and all the passengers and crew could do was wait and hope that another ship would pass close by and take her in tow. Fortunately, that is exactly what happened, and it was the Leyland steamer *William Cliff* which turned out to be the *Etruria*'s saving angel. She towed the Cunard liner to the Azores, and naturally received a generous reward for this service. At that time there were no repair facilities in the Azores, and *Etruria* eventually had to be towed back to Liverpool by tugs, where the damage could be examined and repaired in dock.

◆◆◆

The *City of New York* off Liverpool.

The First Twin-Screw Express Steamers

The Inman & International Line 1889 to 1893

◆◆◆

IN 1889, fourteen years after the triumphant success of the *City of Berlin*, the Inman Line managed to climb back to the peak of international shipping, albeit for the last time. In the mid-1880s the company was threatened with bankruptcy, a fate from which it was saved only by being sold to the International Navigation Company. This was an American enterprise which operated the Belgian-British-American Red Star Line, and under its wing the Inman Line was renamed the Inman & International Steamship Company in November 1886. However, to the outside world the line was still known by its familiar abbreviation.

In 1887 the Inman Line ordered two ships from J & G Thomson in Glasgow, which, without fear of exaggeration, represented a new era in shipbuilding and engine construction. These ships represented a master stroke by the chief designer John Biles. When the *City of New York* came into service in August 1888, followed by her sister ship the *City of Paris* in April 1889, they really were superlative vessels in every respect. They were the world's first twin-screw express liners, and they surpassed their predecessors in absolutely every way—in size, power, speed, passenger comfort and safety. Even those design features of the ships which might be considered antiquated— such as the clipper prow, the three funnels and the three masts— endowed the ships with an inimitable elegance. These ships for the first time incorporated all three of the most significant new developments, refined to a new level of sophistication: the triple-expansion engine, the twin-screw system, and the characteristics of the new material, steel. In addition, by 1887, when that old white elephant, the *Great Eastern*, had finally been sold off to be broken up, the new ships could also be described as the largest ships in the world.

On trials the *City of New York* achieved 20.1 knots, while her sister beat this figure with 21.9 knots. In fact, the ships were exactly identical, and were powered by identical engines, but the *City of Paris* produced around 1500ihp more power, and in terms of speed she was always superior. The reasons for this difference have never been researched or explained. While the *City of New York* had to be satisfied with records in the easterly direction, the *City of Paris* won the coveted Blue Riband, and even managed to improve on her performance in this contest no less than four times.

In her very first year of service the *City of Paris* suffered a spectacular accident which undoubtedly delighted the operators of conventional single-screw express steamers, and raised doubts in the more sceptical minds regarding the safety of twin-screw propulsion. For example, the Bremen-based North German Lloyd company used this accident later to justify its own mis-guided shipbuilding policy°. The accident was certainly a nasty one. On 25 March 1890, on her return crossing to Liverpool, the starboard propeller shaft of the *City of Paris* broke when running at full speed in mid-Atlantic. The engine, now spinning under no-load conditions, simply tore itself apart, the shards piercing the outer skin and unfortunately also the longitudinal bulkhead leading to the port engine room. Water flooded into both engine compartments, which shut down the port engine too. This modern, twin-screw steamer was now reduced to drifting helplessly on the high seas, before eventually being towed in to Queenstown. Of course, this unusual accident did not represent a serious argument against twin-screw propulsion, since the

James R Thomson built the first twin-screw express steamer in 1888.

°Cf Kludas, Arnold, 'Die deutschen Schnelldampfer', *Deutsches Schiffahrtsarchiv*, 3.1990, p152

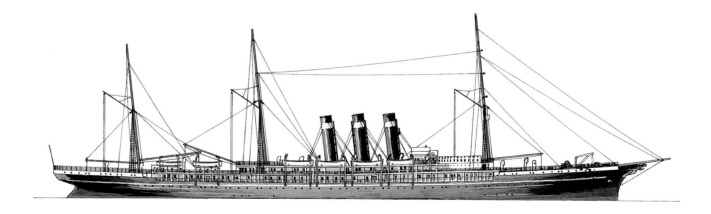

advantages so obviously outweighed the disadvantages. First, if one screw shaft breaks, if a propeller is lost or if an engine fails, the ship still has the second shaft, and can still be manoeuvred. Second, if the rudder is lost, the ship can still be steered by means of the two screws. In later accidents at sea, involving different ships, these advantages became clear, whereas the unfortunate interplay of factors which made this accident so serious never occurred again.

ss *City of New York*

Owner: Inman Line, Liverpool.

Builder: J & G Thomson, Glasgow; Yard No. 240.

Specification: 10,499grt / 560ft overall length / 63ft beam / two triple-expansion engines; Thomson / 18,500ihp / two screws / 20 knots / 540 first-class, 200 second-class, 1000 third-class passengers.

Career: 15.3.1888 launched / 1.8.1888 maiden voyage Liverpool–Queenstown–New York / 5.1889 record crossing in easterly direction / 22.2.1893 renamed *New York*, American Line, New York. 10,508grt. Passengers: 290 first-class, 250 second-class, 725 third-class / 25.2.1893 first voyage New York–Southampton / 4. to 12.1898 US Navy auxiliary cruiser *Harvard* in Spanish-American war / 1898 renamed *New York*

again, American Line / 11.1.1899 returned to New York–Southampton service / 5.1901 to 4.1903 to Cramp, Philadelphia, for refit. 10,798grt, two funnels, new triple-expansion engines / 1913 first-class became second-class / 14.8.1914 first voyage New York–Liverpool / 1918 renamed *Plattsburg*, US transport ship; second mast removed / 1919 again *New York* / 19.2.1920 first voyage New York–Plymouth–Southampton / 1921 to Polish Navigation Co, New York / 14.9.1921 one voyage New York–Antwerp–Danzig and back, then impounded / 1922 to Irish-American Line, 1922 to United Transatlantic Line, no voyages / 10.6.1922 one voyage New York–Naples–Constantinople, there auctioned at orders of US government / 1923 broken up in Genoa.

ss *City of Paris*

Owner: Inman Line, Liverpool.

Builder: J & G Thomson, Glasgow; Yard No. 241.

Specification: 10,499grt / 560ft overall length / 63ft beam / two triple-expansion engines; Thomson / 18,500ihp / two screws / 20 knots / 540 first-class, 200 second-class, 1000 third-class passengers.

Career: 20.10.1888 launched / 3.4.1889 maiden voyage Liverpool–Queenstown–New York / 5.1889 won Blue Riband at 19.95 knots, later improved repeatedly / 5.1889 record crossing in easterly direction / 25.3.1890 propeller shaft fracture, unable to manoeuvre, towed to Queenstown / 13.5.1891 in service again after repair / 2.1893 renamed *Paris*, American Line, New York. 10,508grt, passengers: 290 first-class, 250 second-class,

725 third-class / 25.3.1893 first voyage New York-Southampton / 5. to 10.1898, US Navy auxiliary cruiser *Yale* in Spanish-American war / 21.5.1899 stranded on the Manacles off Cornwall / 11.7.1899 salvaged, repaired in Milford Haven, then to Belfast for refit. 10,786grt, two funnels, new quadruple-expansion engines / 31.8.1901 returned to service as *Philadelphia* / 1913 first-class became second / 19.8.1914 first crossing New York–Liverpool / 1918 became *Harrisburg*, US troop transport ship, second mast removed / 1919 renamed *Philadelphia* again / 12.3.1920 first post-war crossing New York–Southampton / 11.1920 laid up / 1922 to New York-Naples SS Co, New York. 10,232grt / 1.7.1922 first voyage New York–Naples, mutiny and unrest, ship arrested in Naples / 1923 broken up in Genoa.

The sister ships *City of New York* and *City of Paris* were the first twin-screw fast steamers and – apart from the *Great Eastern* – the first passenger ships of more than 10,000grt.

The First German Twin-Screw Fast Steam Ships

◆◆◆

IN THIS chapter, another short digression from the main narrative, we look at a group of ships which have been celebrated in many German publications for a hundred years as the first German liners to hold the Blue Riband—an entirely erroneous claim. The ships in question are the four fast steamers of the *Augusta Victoria* class belonging to the Hamburg-America line, which entered service in the years 1889 to 1891.

The type ship of this class, the *Augusta Victoria*, was the first express liner to be built in a German yard, and when she was launched in 1888 she ranked as the world's second twin-screw liner—only a few months after the *City of New York*. These two impressive facts attracted much attention, and the ships ushered the Hapag company into the leading group of international North Atlantic shipping companies for the first time.

These Hapag steamers were employed on the Hamburg–Southampton–New York route, plying the Channel run, and competing with North German Lloyd and the French Cie Gén Transatlantique. Right from the outset these ships pushed the Lloyd steamers out of the top places which they had held in the statistics of the US Postmaster for the mail run times between New York and London. However, they never gained the distinction of the Blue Riband. Although they were the fastest ships between the English Channel and New York in their time, the Blue

The Hapag steamers of the *Augusta Victoria* class were two of the world's first twin-screw fast steam ships. *Augusta Victoria,* shown here, was also the first fast steamer to be built at a German shipyard, the Stettin-based Vulcan yard.

Riband was held by the British fast steamers running between Liverpool and New York. As I wrote before, it is easy to see how slightly ambiguous press reports and promotional brochures have mislead readers and historians alike.[°]

How is it possible that announcements of the fastest Atlantic crossings could reach the press, and eventually the literature, without them ever taking place? One reason is the fact that the US mail administration listed the Hapag ships as the fastest mail steamers, and this was enough to lead a layman to believe that they were necessarily the fastest ships in the world. And this view was confirmed precisely by the reports that the layman could read in the newspapers. A promotional brochure from Hapag[°°] printed in 1892 quoted a number of announcements. For example, on 20 May 1889 the *New York Herald Tribune* published the following report after the maiden voyage of the *Augusta Victoria*: 'An ocean record smashed. The fastest maiden trip westward. Splendid promise made by the new steamship *Augusta Victoria*.' The fact that this story proclaimed—quite rightly—the world's fastest maiden voyage, but not the fastest Atlantic crossing of all time, was not understood by every contemporary newspaper. The following story from the British *Star* of 17 October 1890 also reported a world record, albeit a different one: 'The Steamship *Columbia* of the Hamburg American Packet Line, which left New York at two p.m. on Oct. 9, reached Southampton yesterday at noon, having beaten the best record ever made between the two ports by two hours and 11 minutes.' Here again no absolute world record is claimed, but simply a record voyage between two ports. When the *Fuerst Bismarck* completed an easterly crossing at an average speed of 19.75 knots, the *Paris Herald*, dated 18 September 1891, wrote the following: 'Thus beating the fastest eastward passage yet made by any steamer.' In this case the claim is unambiguous, and asserts an absolute world record, but at this time the real record was actually held by the *City of Paris*. All these stories are based on press information issued by Hapag; the content of this information was correct, but was mis-interpreted by journalists, albeit with the best of intentions. Naturally, not all journalists and authors were familiar with global shipping; not everyone knew that the British were running ships between Liverpool and New

York which were half a knot faster than the German liners. These writers therefore wrote what they considered to be the truth; and since the shipping company found the mistakes to be promotionally effective, it could see no reason to correct them.

Although none of these four ships ever held the Blue Riband, they still earned a notable place in shipping history. In 1889 they were at the starting point of that successful path which in ten years took the Hamburg-America Line from 22nd place in the world rankings to the very top position amongst the world's greatest shipping companies.

The steamers of the Augusta-Victoria class (printed bold) compared with their international competitors

Name	Shipping company	First voyage	grt	knots[°]	Passengers		
					1st	2nd	Steerage
CITY OF NEW YORK	Inman	1. Aug 1888	10499	20	540	200	1000
CITY OF PARIS	Inman	3. Apr 1889	10449	20	540	200	1000
AUGUSTA VICTORIA	Hapag	10. May 1889	7661	18	400	120	580
COLUMBIA	Hapag	18. Jul 1889	7578	18	400	120	580
TEUTONIC	White Star	7. Aug 1889	9984	19	300	190	1000
MAJESTIC	White Star	2. Apr 1890	9965	19	300	190	1000
NORMANNIA	Hapag	22. May 1890	8716	19	420	172	700
FÜRST BISMARCK	Hapag	8. May 1891	8874	19	420	172	700
LA TOURAINE	C.G.T.	20. Jun 1891	8893	19	392	98	600
CAMPANIA	Cunard	22. Apr 1893	12950	21	600	400	1000
LUCANIA	Cunard	2. Sep 1893	12952	21	600	400	1000

[°]Service speed in knots

The C G T and Hapag ships took the English Channel route; the British steamers ran from Liverpool to New York.

[°]In 1981 and again subsequently in my *Geschichte der deutschen Passagierchiffahrt* (Vol 1, p188) I have expressed my opinion on this complex subject in detail, and proved my theses. Cf Kludas, Arnold, 'Die deutschen Schnelldampfer' *Deutsches Schiffahrtsarchiv*, vol 4, 1981, p96

[°°]*Across the Atlantic* (Hamburg 1892) p10

The *Normannia* built in Great Britain in 1890, shown here in an atmospheric oil painting by the Bremen-American maritime artist Fred Pansing.

A Final Interlude

The White Star Line, 1891 to 1892

◆◆◆

IN 1887 the White Star Line's leading ships were still the two express liners *Britannic* and *Germanic* built in 1874/75, but after twelve years in service they no longer justified this title. As early as 1885 Sir Edward Harland had reminded his friend Thomas Ismay, over the dinner table, that the White Star Line had not ordered any express liners for a long time, despite the rapid technical progress of the period. Ismay knew that Harland was right, but there were good reasons why Ismay had not acted earlier, namely, that having watched the latest belligerent developments in the Balkans, and the role which Russian auxiliary cruisers had played in it, he had begun negotiations with the British Admiralty. His suggestion was that he should design his fast liners in such a way that they could easily be employed later as auxiliary cruisers, and made available for war in the shortest possible time, should an emergency arise. The Admiralty officials were delighted with this idea, and declared themselves ready to pay the cost of such installations, as well as the cost of keeping the ships in a state of readiness.°

Once this had been settled, in the spring of 1887, there was nothing to delay granting a contract for two new fast liners to the house yard of Harland & Wolff. Although it was stipulated that these ships were not to be inferior to the Inman liners, which had been ordered virtually at the same time, in all other respects the yard was given

In 1899 the White Star Line commissioned her last express liner in the shape of the 17,272grt *Oceanic*, built by Harland & Wolff in Belfast in 1899. The largest ship in the world when commissioned, she was never intended to break records; instead her task was to provide a weekly transatlantic service together with the *Majestic* and *Teutonic*.

Profile of the *Teutonic* of 1889.

°Anderson, Roy, *White Star Line* (Prescot 1964) p77

With the *Teutonic* (shown here) and her sister ship the *Majestic*, the White Star Line made its last attempt to win the Blue Riband.

carte blanche in their design. The *Teutonic* was delivered in July 1889, and was immediately fitted out as an auxiliary cruiser so that it could take part in the great Naval Review at Spithead scheduled for 1 August. The auxiliary cruiser attracted due attention from the foreign guests, not least from Kaiser Wilhelm II. He was shown over the ship by Ismay and the Prince of Wales –the later King Edward VII–and was clearly impressed. Virtually all the great seafaring nations adopted this new idea.

However, on 7 August 1889 the *Teutonic* resumed her true vocation by setting off on her maiden voyage to New York. Her sister ship *Majestic* followed in April 1890. The ships were just short of 10,000 tons gross and had been designed by A H Carlisle. The new liners were quite up to the standard of the Inman ships, although in external appearance they were entirely different, in the sense that they looked more functional with their straight stems. The *Teutonic* and *Majestic* were also among

The *Majestic* won the Blue Riband in August 1890, but held it for just fourteen days.

the first liners whose masts were no longer fitted with yards. Both ships won the Blue Riband, in July and August 1891 respectively. One year later the Inman sister ships regained the Blue Riband, and thereafter the White Star Line never made further record attempts. White Star's future policy became to build large luxury liners with moderate speed – the most famous of these was, in 1912, the *Titanic*.

Profile of *Majestic* of 1890.

SS *Teutonic*

Owner: White Star Line, Liverpool.

Builder: Harland & Wolff, Belfast; Yard No. 208.

Specification: 9,984grt / 582ft overall length / 57.8ft beam / two triple-expansion engines; Harland & Wolff / 17,500ihp / two screws / 20 knots / 300 first-class, 190 second-class, 1000 third-class passengers.

Career: 19.1.1889 launched / 1.8.1889 participated as auxiliary cruiser in Naval Review at Spithead / 7.8.1889 maiden voyage Liverpool – Queenstown – New York / 13. to 19.8.1891 won Blue Riband at 20.35 knots / 12.6.1907 first voyage Southampton – Cherbourg – New York / 13.5.1911 first voyage Liverpool – Quebec – Montreal. Passengers now: 550 second-class, 1000 third-class / 20.9.1914 auxiliary cruiser, Tenth Cruiser Squadron / 16.8.1915 sold to the Admiralty / 1918 troop transport ship / 1921 laid up in Cowes / 1921 broken up at Emden.

SS *Majestic*

Owner: White Star Line, Liverpool.

Builder: Harland & Wolff, Belfast; Yard No. 209.

Specification: 9,965grt / 582ft overall length / 57.8ft beam / two triple-expansion engines; Harland & Wolff / 17,500ihp / two screws / 20 knots / 300 first-class, 190 second-class, 1000 third-class passengers.

Career: 29.6.1889 launched / 2.4.1890 maiden voyage Liverpool – Queenstown – New York / 30.7 to 5.8.1891 won Blue Riband at 20.10 knots / 12.1899 to 3.1900 troop transport ship, Boer War / 1902 to 1903 refit at Harland & Wolff in Belfast. 10,147grt, new boilers, longer funnels, second mast removed / 26.6.1907 first voyage Southampton – Cherbourg – New York / 1911 laid up as reserve ship, reactivated after sinking of *Titanic* / 17.10.1913 rescued crew of sinking French schooner *Garonne* / 1.1914 out of service / 5.5.1914 to Morecambe for breaking up.

Alone at the Top Again
The Cunard Line, 1893 to 1897

◆◆◆

AFTER 1890 the contest for the Blue Riband began to intensify, and Cunard realised that the *Umbria* and *Etruria*, which were just six years old, would soon have to be replaced by expensive new liners if the company wanted to remain in the top group of North Atlantic shipping companies. Of course, there was absolutely no question that Cunard wanted to maintain its status. The fact that the Guion Line and now Inman were no longer taking part in the competition did not ease the situation in any way, for though the firm's British rivals were now eliminated, foreign shipping companies were forming up for the first time as candidates for speed record attempts. The Germans in particular were making rapid progress, and – as mentioned earlier – the Hamburg-America Line had been the second to commission twin-screw express steamers, at the same time as Inman but before White Star.

It was clear that the Cunard Line now also had to adopt twin-screw technology as quickly as possible. In 1891 the company granted a contract for building two fast 13,000grt ships. The recipient was the Fairfield Shipbuilding & Engineering Company of Glasgow, the successor company to the Elder concern. The size of these ships alone is ample evidence of the momentum which was building up at this time, and this drive to increase the size of steamers had been made possible by the adoption of steel as hull material in 1887. In terms of passenger appointments both ships were also in the very forefront of comfort. They were the first liners to include single cabins; the

Contemporary engraving of the
Lucania.

The Cunard Line was the last of the leading North Atlantic shipping companies to build twin-screw liners; the picture shows the *Campania* in the river Mersey.

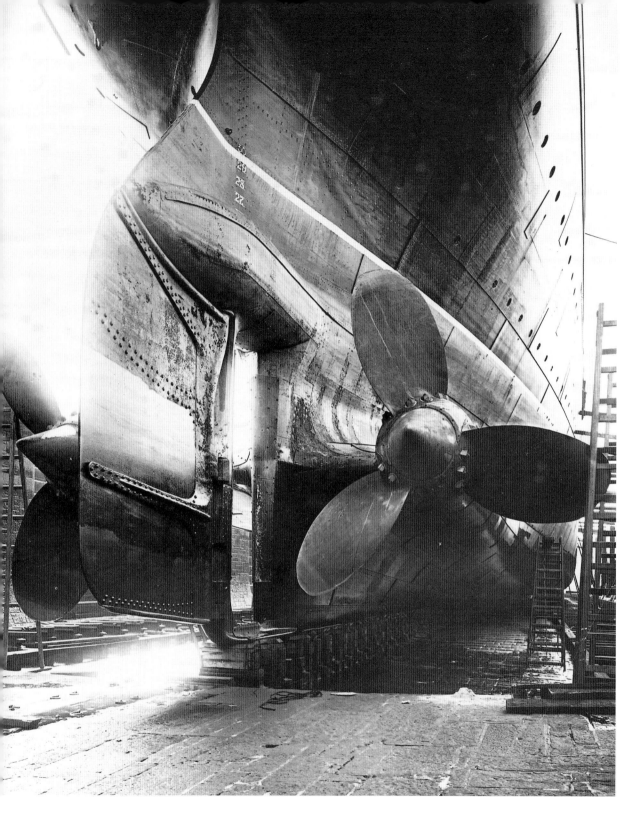

Above: The *Campania* in the Mersey prior to her maiden voyage.

Left: An impressive photograph of the stern of the *Campania* showing the rudder blade and the twin propellers.

Opposite page: The first-class dining hall of the *Campania*, pictured here set up as a drawing-room between mealtimes. Note the heaters under the tables, and the Cunard lions carved into the backrests of the swivel chairs.

children in the first-class cabins had their own dining room; there were open fires in the lounge and smoking saloon, and the perishable provisions were stored in large refrigerated rooms.

Both ships entered service in 1893, and the *Campania* duly won the Blue Riband in June of that year with an average speed of 21.12 knots; the first time the record had stood above 21 knots. The *Lucania* overtook her sister ship that same year, and by 1894 the record had risen to 21.81 knots. In the opposite direction the *Lucania* even managed to set a speed of just on 22 knots in 1895. To achieve this figure, which surpassed the performance of the *City of Paris* by 1.11 knots, the *Lucania* had to produce an extra 10,000ihp, 30,000 instead of 20,000. To manage this, the 132 stokers on the fireroom staff had to shift 560 tons of coal per day, shovelling it incessantly into the 96 furnaces. And for all this effort the *Lucania* reached New York just one hour and thirteen minutes earlier than the older ship. Certainly this performance was achieved at the cost of complete disregard for economic considerations.

Profile of the *Campania* of 1893.

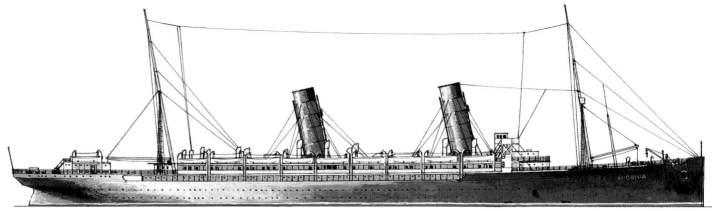

Profile of the *Lucania* of 1893.

ss *Campania*

Owner: Cunard Line, Liverpool.

Builder: Fairfield Shipbuilding and Engineering Co, Glasgow; Yard No. 364.

Specification: 12,950grt / 622ft overall length / 65ft beam / two five-cylinder triple-expansion engines; Fairfield / 30,000ihp / two screws / 21 knots / 600 first-class, 400 second-class, 1000 third-class passengers / crew 415.

Career: 8.9.1892 launched / 22.4.1893 maiden voyage Liverpool–Queenstown–New York / 5.1893 record voyage in easterly direction / 6.1894 won Blue Riband at 21.12 knots, 1894 improved to 21.44 knots / 1894 collided with bark *Embleton* in St George's Channel in fog; *Embleton* cut in two, sank with eleven men / 23.5

to 20.6.1914 first of two voyages Glasgow–New York on charter to the Anchor Line / 15.10.1914 sold for breaking up / 27.11.1914 to Admiralty, rebuilt as aircraft carrier at Cammell, Laird & Co, Birkenhead / 4.1916 commissioned / 5.11.1918 drove against prow of battleship *Revenge* when anchor chain failed in a storm. Holed, sunk.

ss *Lucania*

Owner: Cunard Line, Liverpool.

Builder: Fairfield Shipbuilding & Engineering Co., Glasgow; Yard No. 365.

Specification: 12,952grt / 622ft overall length / 65ft beam / two five-cylinder triple-expansion engines; Fairfield / 30,000ihp / two screws / 21 knots / 600 first-class, 400 second-class, 1000 third-class passengers / crew 415.

Career: 2.2.1893 launched / 2.9.1893 maiden voyage Liverpool–Queenstown–New York / 8.1894 won Blue Riband at 21.65 knots, improved twice later / 1894/95 three record crossings in easterly direction / 7.1909 laid up in Liverpool / 14.8.1909 burned out in Liverpool. Under own power to Swansea, broken up.

The Decade of the Germans

◆◆◆

THE YEAR 1897 marked the end of one era in the contest for the Blue Riband, and ushered in a new one. In September 1897 the *Kaiser Wilhelm der Grosse* left Bremerhaven for her maiden voyage to New York. The commissioning of this ship introduced a new period in the history of international shipping. Since the beginnings of the steam ship Great Britain had exerted an unchallenged dominance over the international scene. The Blue Riband had also been in the hands of the British throughout this period, particularly so if we include the Anglo-American Collins, whose ships had held the record from 1850 to 1856. Now, for the first, time another nation proved to be capable of matching and surpassing the achievements of the British; in this case the Germans, who were showing that they were the primary competitor to Britain in all areas of the economy. This fundamental rivalry pushed the battle for the Blue Riband into much starker relief, as it became an international competition where national prestige itself was at stake. The perception that something new and special was happening is clear from the more intensive reporting of the Blue Riband at this time. The subject became extremely popular in the press, and this was the time when the term 'Blue Riband' itself first came into popular usage.

At this time in Germany there were two major transatlantic shipping companies: the Hamburg-based Hamburg-Amerikanische Packetfahrt-Actien-Gesellschaft and in Bremen the Norddeutscher Lloyd. The first company was generally abbreviated as 'Hapag', and widely known by its short name, the Hamburg-American line; the Bremen company, which had been founded in 1857, was often known simply as Lloyd or NDL.

NORTH GERMAN LLOYD, 1898 TO 1903

Between 1881 and 1891 the Lloyd company had built up the world's largest fleet of international express steamers comprising eleven ships (pages 63-66), and with two departures per week their transatlantic service represented the most regular line network on that route. In establishing this service the Bremen-based Lloyd had climbed to the top of the international passenger statistics for all the Europe-USA lines. This story of success can be attributed to the Lloyd director Lohmann, although he did subsequently exhibit remarkable obstinacy in keeping faith

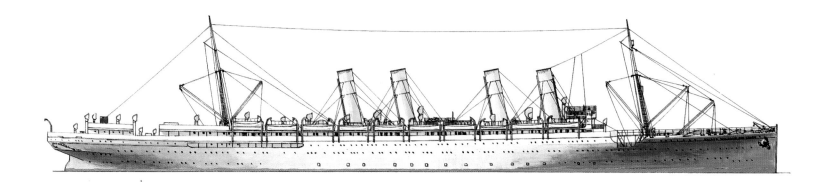

Profile of the *Kaiser Wilhelm der Grosse* of 1897.

The express liner *Kaiser Wilhelm der Grosse*. Her commissioning in 1897 ushered in the 'Decade of the Germans' in the North Atlantic.

with the single-screw principle long after the superiority of the twin-screw ship had been proved beyond doubt. When Lohmann died, his successor Heinrich Wiegand found himself faced with a difficult quandary. The Hapag company represented Lloyd's most dangerous rival, not least due to its location in nearby Hamburg. Since Hapag had already procured a modern fleet of twin-screw liners, Lloyd's leading position was clearly

in jeopardy. Wiegand took the bold option, and in 1895 he ordered two new twin-screw steamers, one from the Vulcan yard in Stettin and the other from Schichau in Danzig. The technical specification of these new vessels placed them firmly in the top echelon of what was possible at that time, and it could be claimed that Lloyd was reaching for the stars. This brave move proved successful, and from 1897 to 1907 the German express

The *Kronprinz Wilhelm* in the roads off Cherbourg. On the right of the picture can be seen a passenger tender at the stern of the vessel, which was used to ferry passengers to the ocean-going ship from the French port.

steamers, with their four funnels grouped in pairs, were the fastest passenger ships in the world. For this reason this period in the history of the Blue Riband became known as 'the decade of the Germans'.

In November 1897 *Kaiser Wilhelm der Grosse* made her first attempt at a record crossing, completing the eastbound voyage from Sandy Hook to the Needles at 22.33 knots. In the spring 1898 the same ship went on to gain the Blue Riband, the first time that it had been

ss *Kaiser Wilhelm der Grosse*

Owner: North German Lloyd, Bremen.

Builder: AG Vulcan, Stettin; Yard No. 234.

Specification: 14,349grt / 6400dwt / 648.5ft overall length / 66ft beam / two four-cylinder triple-expansion engines; Vulcan / 27,000ihp / two screws / 22 knots / 206 first-class, 226 second-class, 1074 third-class passengers / crew 488.

Career: 4.5.1897 launched / 19.9.1897 maiden voyage Bremerhaven – Southampton – New York / 11.1897 record voyage in easterly direction / 30.3 to 5.4.1898 won Blue Riband at 22.29 knots / 21.1.1906 collided with British steamer *Orinoco* off Cherbourg; three seamen and five passengers killed / 1913 to 1914 refit as emigrant ship. 13,952grt, 630 third-class, 1500 steerage passengers / 2.8.1914 auxiliary cruiser, Imperial Navy / 22.8.1914 engaged by British cruiser *Highflyer* during coal transfer off Rio del Oro, Spanish West Africa. After the Germans had exhausted their munitions, they opened the flood valves and scuttled the ship.

ss *Kronprinz Wilhelm*

Owner: North German Lloyd, Bremen.

Builder: AG Vulcan, Stettin; Yard No. 249.

Specification: 14,908grt / 6900dwt / 663.3ft overall length / 66.2ft beam / two six-cylinder quadruple-expansion engines; Vulcan / 33,000ihp / two screws / 22.5 knots / 301 first-class, 300 second-class, 717 third-class passengers / crew 528.

Career: 30.3.1901 launched / 17.9.1901 maiden voyage Bremerhaven – Southampton – Cherbourg – New York / 10. to 16.9.1902 won Blue Riband at 23.09 knots / 8.10.1902 collision in fog in English Channel with British freighter *Robert Ingham*, on which two died / 3.8.1914 left New York to rendezvous with cruiser *Karlsruhe*, fitted out at sea as auxiliary cruiser / 6.8.1914 commissioned / 10.4.1915 entered Newport News, interned / 6.4.1917 requisitioned by USA / 9.6.1917 renamed *Von Steuben*, US Navy transport ship / 1919 to US Shipping Board, New York / 1923 to Boston for breaking up.

ss *Kaiser Wilhelm II*

Owner: North German Lloyd, Bremen.

Builder: AG Vulcan, Stettin; Yard No. 250

Specification: 19,341grt / 8700dwt / 706.5ft overall length / 72.3ft beam / four quadruple-expansion engines; Vulcan / 38,000ihp / two screws / 22.5 knots / 468 first-class, 268 second-class, 799 third-class passengers / crew 650.

Career: 12.8.1902 launched / 14.4.1903 maiden voyage Bremerhaven – Southampton – Cherbourg – New York / 6.1904 record voyage in easterly direction / 17.6.1914 rammed by British freighter *Incemore* off Southampton / by 28.7.1914 repaired by Harland & Wolff in Southampton / 8.1914 laid up in New York due to war situation / 6.4.1917 requisitioned by USA / 5.9.1917 renamed *Agamemnon*, US Navy transport ship / 1919 to US Shipping Board, New York. Laid up / 1929 renamed *Monticello*. Norfolk, later laid up in Patuxent River/1940 to Boston for breaking up.

Heinrich Wiegand (1855-1909), Managing Director of the North German Lloyd company, and initiator of the German four-funnel express steamers.

The attempt by the Danzig Schichau yard to build a top-level express steamer ended in a technical disaster. The *Kaiser Friedrich* was intended to be a running mate for the *Kaiser Wilhelm der Grosse*, but no amount of modification was able to bring her up to the specified speed of 22 knots, with the result that North German Lloyd rejected the 12,481grt ship and returned her to the yard in 1898.

A contemporary postcard intended to illustrate the size of current ocean liners by comparing them with familiar buildings or squares. Such cards were very popular for a while.

Norddeutscher Lloyd, Bremen.

Doppelschrauben-Schnellpostdampfer „Kaiser Wilhelm II" auf dem Augustusplatz in Leipzig.
Dampferlänge 215 m. Länge des Augustusplatzes (Museum bis Theater) 218 m. Dampferhöhe bis zum Bootsdeck 21,25 m, mit den Schornsteinen 41 m. Höhe des Museums (bis obere Attika) 19 m. Höhe des Neuen Theaters (bis obere Attika) 32 m.

held by a German ship. In so doing the Lloyd steamer improved the record from 21.81 to 22.29 knots, thereby exceeding the 22-knot mark for the first time. Another 'first' was the designation of the Needles, the rocky chalk outcrops to the west of the Isle of Wight, as a new destination for the record crossing. Whereas Liverpool and Queenstown had formerly been the eastern measurement points, the German ships used a location in the English Channel for their record attempts.

The maiden voyage of the second express liner proved to be a gigantic disappointment to NDL as well as to the yard which had built it. *Kaiser Friedrich* could only manage the paltry speed of 20 knots, and all attempts at improvement by the Schichau yard came to nothing. The contract stipulated a speed of 22 knots, and as this was not achieved Lloyd invoked its right of cancellation and returned the three-funnel steamer to the yard. At this time the company placed an order with Stettin-based Vulcan for a sister ship to the successful four-funnel liner, but this vessel could not be delivered until 1901. This delay gave its rival Hapag the opportunity to gain a lead of a year with its own four-funnel fast steamer the *Deutschland*.

The library and writing room of the *Kronprinz Wilhelm*.

The ladies' room and writing room on the *Kaiser Wilhelm der Grosse*.

The first-class smoking saloon on the *Kaiser Wilhelm der Grosse*.

The *Kaiser Wilhelm der Grosse* enters New York showing clearly the scars of a stormy Atlantic crossing.

North German Lloyd's Pier No. 1 in Hoboken, New Jersey. The pier was on the Hudson river, facing New York City.

Kaiser Wilhelm der Grosse had set new standards for this class of ship, and the *Deutschland* in turn surpassed her predecessor by a clear margin, but it then became difficult for further ships of this type to set new records. The *Kronprinz Wilhelm* of the NDL undertook her first voyage in August 1901. She was very similar to the first ship, and only slightly enlarged, and her quadruple-expansion engines produced almost as much power as the Hapag ship. A year later *Kronprinz Wilhelm* succeeded in relieving the *Deutschland* of the Blue Riband, but the *Deutschland* managed to regain it in September 1903.

The fourth ship of this type was the *Kaiser Wilhelm II* belonging to NDL, which was built in 1903. At almost 20,000grt she

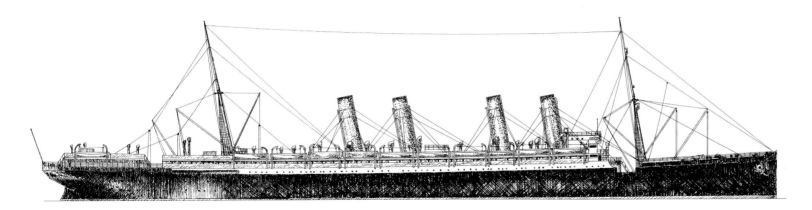

Profile of the *Kronprinz Wilhelm* of 1901.

The *Kaiser Wilhelm II* was built in 1903, and although 5,000grt larger than the first four-funnel ships, she was only able to set a new record for an eastbound voyage.

The Hapag express steamer *Deutschland* in July 1900, shown during her departure from the port of New York.

was 25 per cent larger than the *Kronprinz Wilhelm*. She was powered by four gigantic quadruple-expansion engines, two working on each shaft, and this installation developed almost 45,000ihp, 9,000 more than the *Kronprinz Wilhelm's* engines could produce. Unfortunately, the greater tonnage outweighed the extra power, with the result that the *Kaiser Wilhelm II* never succeeded in winning the Blue Riband. In recompense she was able to set a new record for the eastbound crossing in 1904, and her average speed of 23.58 knots was not beaten until the *Lusitania* made her record run in 1907.

In 1907 North German Lloyd commissioned its last four-funnel vessel, the *Kronprinzessin Cecilie*, a sister ship to the *Kaiser Wilhelm II*. However, this steamer never took part in the contest for the Blue Riband, and in any case only a few weeks later the latest British express steamers resumed their domination of the competition.

THE HAMBURG-AMERICA LINE, 1900 TO 1907

In 1889 the Hamburg-America Line was the second shipping company in the world to have commissioned twin-screw liners (pages 74-76), and by 1891 possessed the largest fleet of this type amongst the major shipping companies. These were the four ships of the *Augusta-Victoria* class. The inspiration to build this class had come from the young Albert Ballin, whose energy was responsible for a remarkable period of growth in the Hapag company. Ten years later the same Albert Ballin had grown to be rather sceptical of the value of the express liner. By that time he had been obliged to watch his four express steamers being over-taken by further technical development within just a few years. The same fate was unavoidable for every liner during this era of breakneck technical development, as companies were discovering world-wide. Building and operating such ships was never the cheapest option, and although their prestige value was high, the economic balance appeared dubious at best.

However, the spectacular reputation which North German Lloyd had made for itself in 1897 with the *Kaiser Wilhelm der Grosse* inflamed the patriotism of the proud inhabitants of Hamburg, and the same feeling was echoed within the company itself. Ignoring the counsel of Ballin, the Hapag board of directors took a bold decision, and the Stettin-based Vulcan yard was granted a contract from Hapag to build a steamer whose specification consisted of a single sentence: the new vessel should surpass the Bremen four-funnel ships in every respect!

This requirement was met by the *Deutschland* in full. The Vulcan yard supplied Hapag with a larger, faster and better version of the Bremen four-funnel liner. On her maiden voyage to New York in July 1900 the *Deutschland* succeeded in gaining the Blue Riband for Hapag, and on the return voyage she immediately broke the record for the opposite direction. The ship improved her performance several times in both directions, proving conclusively that she was the fastest of the five German four-funnel ships. The *Deutschland* also held the Blue Riband for longer than all the other German ships.

In Great Britain the appearance of the *Deutschland* triggered passionate debate and much controversy. The Germans had now held the Blue Riband for three years, and although the failure of the white elephant *Kaiser Friedrich* raised British spirits slightly, they sank again even further when the *Deutschland* broke all records on her very first round-trip. A commentator in the British specialist journal *The Engineer*** wrote a fair and well-informed report, coloured with a good portion of humour, warning that it was illusory to imagine that British liners only now needed to steam at high speed in order to win back the record; he also wagged a finger at those who believed that all the British had to do was wait 'until the Germans shook the rivets out of their steamers in their craving for records', and thereby exclude themselves from the competition. To some in the British shipping industry, who had expressed the opinion that they should not even try to go faster in the interests of safety, *The Engineer* argued that, first, this was simply the way of all progress, and second, that one or two knots more would not constitute a safety risk. The commentator was evidently convinced that the British would again lead the field, but at the time his opinion was 'that the game does not pay'.

The Engineer returned to the subject in September 1900 by printing a supplement to the article quoted above. The occasion was the legendary race between the *Kaiser Wilhelm der Grosse* and the *Deutschland* in September 1900, when the NDL liner left New York one and a half hours before the *Deutschland*. The following day the Hapag steamer had her Bremen rival in her sights, and to the delight of the *Deutschland*'s passengers she pulled past the *Kaiser Wilhelm der Grosse*, with both ships running at full power and with the lively participation of the passengers on both ships. After the ships' arrival in Southampton, a journalist on *The Engineer* interviewed the officers of the two liners, who vehemently denied that a race had taken place at all. The commentator quoted an old Thames skipper's doggerel 'We ain't a racing where the craft are thickest, we're only trying which can go the quickest'. The commentator further remarked that at least Mr Howden would very likely have enjoyed the success of the *Deutschland*, whose boiler rooms were fitted with the artificial draught system patented by Howden which forced the fires, while the officers of the Bremen-based *Kaiser* could claim that their speed would have been higher had a stronger head wind blown into the air inlet hoods.

Although the *Deutschland*'s performance was impressive, there was a high price to pay for it, and not only in terms of invoices from the coal suppliers. At high speed, and she was built to run at high speed, she generated severe vibration. This characteristic earned the *Deutschland* the less than flattering nickname 'the cocktail shaker'. As if this were not enough, on 22 April 1902 the *Deutschland* lost her rudder in heavy seas on the

Albert Ballin (1857-1918), whose determination took the Hamburg-American Line to the peak of all the world's shipping companies.

---

*24 August 1900 issue, p185, in the article 'The Atlantic Record'.

An atmospheric promotional picture of the *Deutschland* on a Hapag calendar.

Hamburg-Amerika Linie

1905

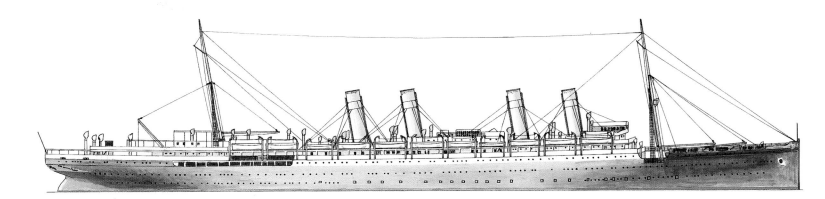

home crossing, 400 nautical miles to the west of Bishop Rock. Captain Albers was able to bring the ship to Cuxhaven in safety, however, steering by means of the twin screws. When the damage was examined more closely, it was clear that the whole stern had suffered damage, in addition to the loss of the rudder, and this damage had undeniably been caused by the constant over-stressing from vibration. Instead of earning money during the high season, the *Deutschland* was now destined for the dock-

Staircase, left, and dining hall, right, in first class on the *Deutschland*.

97

yards for protracted repairs and improvements. When finally she returned to service, it was found that the old problem of vibration was hardly any better.

These events confirmed Ballin's earlier scepticism of the benefits of express steamers, and at this point Hapag abandoned its plan to build a sister ship, renouncing for ever the costly battle for the Blue Riband. Following the lead of the White Star Line, Hapag decided to concentrate on the large, luxurious liner, onboard of which passengers could enjoy a comfortable crossing without vibration, and indulge in the comforts offered for one or two extra days.

It is appropriate here to discuss the question of state subsidies as it has so often been claimed that the North Atlantic services of the Hamburg-America Line and North German Lloyd were supported by massive subsidies from the German Reich, and that, in addition, Kaiser Wilhelm influenced the business policies of both shipping companies on a virtually constant basis. In fact, these claims are so widespread that even renowned authors have taken them for granted.[*]

It should be stressed that, in contrast to several shipping companies which have already been discussed, the German North Atlantic shipping companies were not subsidised. Hapag and Lloyd were certainly reimbursed for carrying mail, but the German shipping companies received no subsidy for adding fittings with military use in mind, such as gun mounts, nor for holding their steamers in readiness for use as auxiliary cruisers. The only state subsidies ever granted were for mail steamer services to Australia and East Asia, the recipients being NDL for the period 1886 to 1914, and Hapag from 1900 to 1903. Never in the Kaiser's reign was state support granted for the North Atlantic service.

It is true that the Kaiser was an enthusiast for matters naval and maritime, and his close contacts with important figures in NDL, and with Hapag's Albert Ballin, are often cited to support the claim that he influenced liner development. Certainly Wilhelm II occasionally became involved in differences between Hapag and Lloyd, but his role was that of the negotiating go-between, intervening only in the way that a teacher does when he attempts to talk sense into two bickering pupils. A good example of this was Wilhelm II's success in settling the dispute between Hapag and Lloyd concerning their proportionate roles as laid down by the Atlantic Conference in 1914[**].

Many writers have picked upon his famous visit to the Spithead Fleet Review in 1889 when his interest in the auxiliary cruiser fittings on the White Star liner *Teutonic*, which Wilhelm wanted to adopt on German liners, led to discussions with his admirals. But there is not a shred of evidence to suggest that he tried to initiate the building programmes of the shipping companies. After all, that programme had already been started in 1887, and by 1889 Hapag had already commissioned two of her first-class, twin-screw express liners; this had been done without the benefit of any Imperial command, and certainly without any subsidy. And in 1889, nobody—neither Lloyd nor Wilhelm II—was even thinking about the four-funnel vessels which the NDL subsequently built.

ss *Deutschland*

Owner: Hamburg-America Line, Hamburg.

Builder: AG Vulcan, Stettin; Yard No. 244.

Specification: 16,502grt / 6908dwt / 684ft overall length / 67.2ft beam / two quadruple-expansion engines; Vulcan / 34,000ihp / two screws / 22.5 knots / 429 first-class, 226 second-class, 284 third-class passengers / crew 557.

Career: 10.1.1900 launched / 4.7.1900 maiden voyage Cuxhaven–New York, winning the Blue Riband at 22.42 knots / also broke the record on the return crossing / all record results subsequently improved repeatedly / 22.4.1902 on the home voyage the *Deutschland* lost her rudder 400 nautical miles west of Bishop Rock in severe weather, but completed the voyage under her own steam / to Blohm & Voss, Hamburg, for repairs; 1902 returned to service / 10.1910 to 9.1911 refitted and renamed as cruise liner *Victoria Luise* at Stettin. 16,703grt, 487 first-class passengers, 15,000ihp, 17.5 knots / 23.9.1911 first cruise / 3.8.1914 re-equipped as auxiliary cruiser in the Imperial Navy; never employed; laid up in Hamburg / 1920 to 10.1.1921 refit at Vulcan yard in Hamburg. 16,333grt, 36 first-class, 1350 third-class passengers, renamed *Hansa* / 27.10.1921 first voyage Hamburg–New York/ 1922: 224 cabin class, 1065 third-class passengers / 28.5.1925 to Hamburg for breaking up.

[*]Maxtone-Graham, John, *The Only Way to Cross* (New York, 1978,) p83, and Brinnin, John Malcolm, *The Sway of the Grand Saloon* (New York 1971,) p306. Two excellent books highly rated by the author

[**]Kludas, Arnold, *Die Geschichte der deutschen Passagierschiffahrt*, (Hamburg 1990) Vol 5, pp24-30

The Third Era: 1907 to 1952
Quadruple-Screw Turbine Express Liners

◆◆◆

Propulsion Technology of the Turbine Steam Ships

IN 1897 Charles Parsons first demonstrated his steam turbine in the form of a marine propulsion system installed in his 44-ton boat *Turbinia*, but long and technically problematic development was necessary before it was mature enough to be employed as a very high performance engine for continuous use in a high-speed steam ship. The turbine's maximum efficiency was reached at very high rotational speeds, whereas the typical ship's propeller was almost over-revving at a speed of only 100rpm (revolutions per minute). At that time it was not possible to manufacture reduction gearboxes of the quality required, so a complex compromise was adopted to match the turbine speed to the speed of the propeller. This required turbine rotors larger than the ideal size, and propellers of different pitch. Considerable experience was gained with turbines fitted to warships and short-distance passenger ships, but a turbine-based power system suitable for long and continuous high-output operation had not even been brought to the testing stage at that time. The first requirement was a six-day Atlantic crossing, and a record voyage with the Blue Riband as target was still some way in the future.

Proven or not, turbines were clearly the engines of the future, and anyone who wanted to carry on competing for the Blue Riband had no option but to gain his own experience with the new technology. In 1905 Cunard made the bold step into the unknown, albeit with government support, and ordered two gigantic turbine-propelled fast steamers, designed to bring the Decade of the Germans to an end. There were no problems with producing the requisite steam pressure,

as the 13.4at required was easy to generate. Of the four ahead turbines two were arranged as high-pressure systems and two as low-pressure ones. Separate astern turbines were installed. The rotational speed of the screws was 180 or 190rpm, more than twice as high as had been used with piston engines.

This was to prove the root cause of a problem which had only just started to manifest itself with the slower revolving screws, namely, cavitation. At 180rpm the propellers thrust the water out astern at such a rate that a vacuum developed in front of the propellers. The vacuum would then be filled by the in-flowing water, producing a massive hammer-like shock. The continual

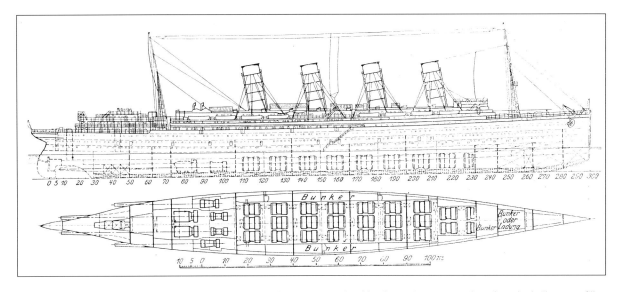

The turbine installation on the *Lusitania*. Limited by the bunkers at one end and by the engine room at the other, the boiler room fills the space below the four funnels. In the engine room are the six turbines, connected directly to the shafts. The high-pressure turbines are on the outside. Towards the stern can be seen the larger housing of the two low-pressure turbines, on the same axis as the inner screw shafts. Forward of these are the two astern turbines, which also act on the inner shafts.

The British engineer Charles (later Sir Charles) Parsons (1854-1931) invented the multi-stage steam turbine, the system which powered all the fast steamers designed in the twentieth century.

blows on the four propellers were transmitted to the shafts in the form of vibration, and the vibration naturally reached the hull. These teething troubles made it necessary, initially, to restrict the ships' speed, with the result that they surpassed the performance of the German steamers by only a relatively narrow margin. Attempts were made to counter this problem by strengthening the aftership, and by 1909 new, four-bladed propellers had been built. The new screws solved the problem, and the ships were now vibration-free and capable of speeds of 26 knots and more. The *Lusitania* and *Mauretania* were the only liners to gain the Blue Riband powered by direct-acting turbines.

By 1929, when the Germans set about winning back the Blue Riband, technical developments had reached the stage where quite different solutions to the problems could be adopted. Modern oil-fired waterpipe boilers could produce a steam pressure of 23at, and the turbines themselves were able to survive running at 1800rpm, instead of being throttled back to 180rpm. Reliable, efficient gearboxes had also been developed, which ensured that the screws were limited to only 180rpm, and the problem of cavitation was well in hand by this time.

Until the advent of the *United States*—the last holder of the Blue Riband—no further fundamental changes were made to marine turbine propulsion systems. The only real development was in maximum boiler steam pressure, which, during the 1930s, rose to 28at, while the high-pressure boilers of the *United States* could generate no less than 68at.

The French *Normandie* represented an exceptional case, as she was fitted with a turbo-electric propulsion system. Her four turbines drove four generators, which produced the electrical current required for the four electric drive motors. There were three primary advantages to this system. The first was that the turbines did not require reduction gearboxes, and therefore were simpler and more efficient. The second was the ship's improved manoeuvring characteristics, as the electric motors, unlike turbines, could be reversed. The third advantage was that the astern turbines were simply not needed.

Another important difference between reciprocating steam engines and turbines must also be borne in mind when assessing and comparing power plants: the different methods of measuring engine power. The measurement unit for turbine output is the Shaft Horse Power (shp), whereas Indicated Horse Power (ihp) is used for piston engines. The ratio of shp to ihp is around four to five, so that the 76,000shp of the *Lusitania* is equivalent to 95,000ihp in a piston-engined vessel. Compared with the 46,000ihp of the piston engines installed in the *Kaiser Wilhelm II* this represents an increase of more than 100 per cent.

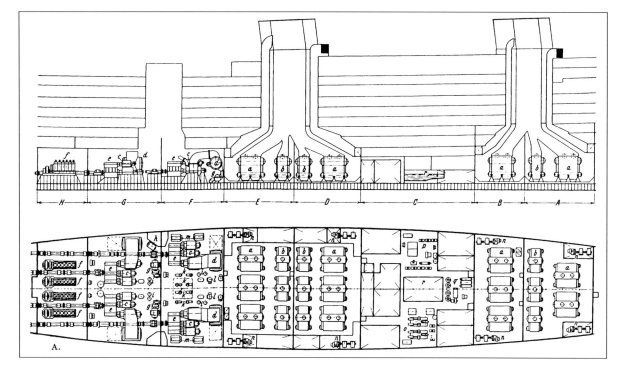

The turbine installation on the *Bremen* clearly illustrates the results of twenty-two years of technical development when compared with the *Lusitania* installation. The high-pressure boilers now take up considerably less space, and the four three-stage turbine sets transmit their power to the propeller shafts via gearboxes; the gearboxes can reverse the direction of rotation of the shaft, thereby eliminating the need for separate astern turbines.

Comeback with Subsidised Technology

The Cunard Line, 1907 to 1929

❖❖❖

ALL THE great North Atlantic shipping companies were eventually obliged to acknowledge that it was a very expensive matter to operate express steamers. The clear reasons for this were the high cost of fuel and the expense of procuring and operating the vessels; less obvious was the fact that crack ships were soon top-notch ships no longer, as their performance and facilities were surpassed by the liners of rival companies. Of course, the latter problem was due in large part to the existence of the Blue Riband competition which the shipping companies themselves promoted. However, there really was little sense in the situation, for though a five-year-old express liner might well have lost its previous edge in top speed, it was by no means just scrap iron. In fact, it was the same first-class ship it always had been, and would remain so for many years, despite the fact that its rival liners now arrived in New York one hour earlier. This fact must have been obvious to all concerned, just as it was clear that the contest for absolute top speed had become uneconomic. Nevertheless, the striving to compete with and surpass one's rivals has always been one of the great driving forces behind human commerce, and the Blue Riband competition was still very much alive.

In 1893, only four years after entering service, the *Campania* and *Lucania* were no longer the world's largest and fastest ships having been superseded by the German four-funnel liners. Even at this time there was much debate about the Blue Riband contest, and the fact that it had become, to a certain extent, a football in a great international game of politics meant that it had turned into a symbol of national stature and excellence. For this very reason the battle would certainly have continued in the usual way without interruption, in the form of an immediate response from the Cunard Line. However, serious technical

The *Lusitania* arriving at New York.

problems prevented this happening in the short-term: the engine systems of the German four-funnel fast steamers had brought the reciprocating steam engine to the peak of its development, and no further progress was possible. It would have been feasible, in technical terms, to build even larger systems of this type, but in economic terms this made no sense at all. A completely new propulsion system was therefore required, and it already existed in the form of the steam turbine. The delay in implementing these engines in liners was due in part to the problems already described with early turbine technology. At

The *Lusitania* on the river Mersey off Liverpool.

The *Mauretania* pictured in 1907 at her departure from the Tyne.

Profile of the fast steamer *Lusitania* of 1907.

this point development was accelerated by certain external influences[°]. The British government had followed the activities of the American banker and railroad magnate John Pierpont Morgan with considerable anxiety; in 1902 he had founded the International Mercantile Marine Company (IMMC) by purchasing seven major transatlantic shipping companies, including the important White Star Line. His combined fleet numbered 133 steam ships measuring 922,110grt: 14 American, 6 Belgian and 113 British vessels. The British press criticised the government's failure to act in the face of such a sell-out of the British merchant fleet and the sale of the White Star Line in particular was considered to be 'a sad blow to British pride'[°°].

In an effort to prevent the last of the major British Atlantic shipping companies becoming involved in the whirlpool of events, the British government granted a contract to Cunard designed to ensure that the company would never cease to be anything but a purely British concern. The decision was made to grant the Cunard Line a loan to the value of £2.5 million for the construction of two large express liners, together with an annual subsidy of £150,000. The conditions of this offer were more than generous, as the annual subsidy was sufficient to pay the interest on the loan, which had been set at the annual rate of 2.74 per cent, and also to pay back the capital over a period of twenty years.[†] As a result, Cunard obtained its new liners at virtually

zero cost to the company. The chairman and the board of directors of the Hamburg-America Line expressed their regret 'that the English government has used the formation of the Trust as an excuse to put an end to the free play of market forces in an area in which German and English shipping companies have until now produced many outstanding achievements without any State assistance, namely in the area of carrying cabin passengers over the North American route, and to shift the basis of competition artificially in favour of a single shipping company by granting a subsidy of previously unprecedented size to the Cunard Steamship Company'.[‡]

The die was now cast, and Cunard was able to undertake the next step forward. In 1903 Cunard ordered the building of the two 20,000-ton ships, *Caronia* and *Carmania*, both capable of 20 knots, with which the company hoped to gain experience in the operation of steam turbines. The first of the ships was fitted with piston engines, the second with turbines. Both ships were com-

---

[°] Kludas, Arnold, *Die Geschichte der deutschen Passagierschiffahrt* vol 3, (Hamburg 1988), p63

[°°] Bonsor, Noel R P, *North Atlantic Seaway*, (Jersey 1978) vol 2, p741

[†] Isherwood, John H, 'The "Lusitania"', in: *Sea Breezes*, vol 34, 1962, pp409-417

[‡] Annual report of the Hamburg-American Line, Hamburg 1902, p5

Profile of the fast steamer *Mauretania* of 1907.

pleted in 1905, and in May of that year Cunard granted the contract for two further large express liners measuring more than 30,000grt.

The two ships were the *Lusitania*, built at John Brown's yard in Clydebank, and the *Mauretania*, constructed at Swan, Hunter & Wigham Richardson in Wallsend-on-Tyne. Both ships were launched in 1906, and in September 1907 the *Lusitania* set off on her maiden voyage, with the *Mauretania* following in November. These were the first British express liners to be

designed in the twentieth century, and the British engineers exploited their advantages to the full. Cunard's competitors now had to accept that these vessels represented a whole series of new superlatives. The *Lusitania* and *Mauretania* were the world's largest ships, the first turbine-powered, high-speed, four-screw steam ships, and the first liners to offer a service speed of 25 knots from their unprecedentedly powerful engines (76,000shp – almost 100,000ihp).

The marine engineers treated their new turbines with the

TS *Lusitania*

Owner: Cunard Line, Liverpool.

Builder: John Brown & Co, Glasgow; Yard No. 367.

Specification: 31,550grt / 10,390dwt / 786ft overall length / 88ft beam / two high-pressure and two low-pressure turbines; Brown / 68,000shp / 25 knots / 563 first-class, 464 second-class, 1138 third-class passengers / crew 802.

Career: 7.6.1906 launched / 7.9.1907 maiden voyage Liverpool–Queenstown–New York / 6. to 10.10.1907 won Blue Riband at 23.99 knots, repeatedly improved until 1909 / in the

same month: record run in easterly direction / 7.5.1915 torpedoed off Irish coast near Old Head of Kinsale by the German U-boat *U20*; sank within 20 minutes after second explosion. 1198 dead. Cause of second explosion proposed by the researcher Ballard as the combustion of coal dust, while the Irish author O'Sullivan assumed the cause to be combustion of 45 tons of aluminium dust carried in the foreship.

TS *Mauretania*

Owner: Cunard Line, Liverpool.

Builder: Swan, Hunter & Wigham Richardson, Newcastle; Yard No. 735.

Specification: 31,938grt / 12,280dwt / 790ft overall length / 88ft beam / two high-pressure and two low-pressure turbines; Wallsend / 68,000shp / 25 knots / 563 first-class, 464 second-class, 1138 third-class passengers/crew 802.

Career: 20.9.1906 launched / 16.11.1907 maiden voyage Liverpool–Queenstown–New York / 26. to 30.9.1909 won Blue Riband at 26.06 knots / record crossings also in

opposite direction / 10.1914 laid up / 6.1915 troop transport / 9.1915 fitted out as military hospital ship / 1916 troop transport again / 28.6.1919 first post-war crossing Southampton–New York / 25.7.1921 severely damaged by fire in Southampton. Repair and conversion to oil in Newcastle yard. 30,696grt. Passengers: 589 first-class, 400 second-class, 767 third-class/25.3.1922 first voyage after refit Southampton–Cherbourg–New York / After 1930 also employed for cruises / 1933 white hull / 4.7.1935 to Rosyth for breaking up.

The *Lusitania* in the Irish Sea in 1911.

When the First World War started, Great Britain cut off Germany from overseas trade by means of an effective naval blockade. On 18 February 1915 Germany responded by declaring the sea area around Great Britain a war zone, in which any enemy ship would be sunk without warning. This intention was proclaimed to potential Cunard Line passengers – whose ship, the *Lusitania*, was at that time the only fast steamer on the passenger service between New York and Liverpool – by means of advertisements in the New York newspapers placed by the German Ambassador in New York. The *Lusitania* departed from New York on 1 May 1915 and headed for Liverpool, carrying 1959 people, including 440 women and 129 children. On 7 May, as she was passing the Old Head of Kinsale lighthouse, the ship was torpedoed by the German submarine *U 20*, whose commander assumed the four black-painted funnels to be those of a troop transport ship. Immediately after the torpedo hit the ship, there followed a further internal explosion which ripped a second gigantic hole in the hull. In less than twenty minutes the *Lusitania* had sunk, taking the lives of 1198 people, almost all of them civilians, including women, children and almost two hundred neutral American citizens. (Painting by W Malchin.)

The French steamer *France* belonging to the Cie Générale Transatlantique, 23,666grt, built in St Nazaire in 1912. Her service speed of almost 24 knots could be surpassed only by the Cunarders *Lusitania* and *Mauretania*.

greatest care, and only increased their power output gradually; anyone who had expected speeds of more than 25 knots on the first crossings was disappointed. It was not until October 1907 that the *Lusitania* gained the Blue Riband for the first time, and her speed of 23.99 knots was still just below the 24-knot mark. However, both ships increased their performance steadily from year to year, and when the *Mauretania* recorded a new Blue Riband record of 26.06 knots in 1909, she set a speed which was to remain unbeaten until 1929.

Until the First World War no other shipping company made any attempt at relieving Cunard of the Blue Riband. In fact, the company's three great rivals responded to the new challenge in different ways. As we have already mentioned, White Star and Hapag had already withdrawn from the Blue Riband around 1900, and they maintained this position. Of course, this did not mean that they were prepared to surrender their former pre-eminence to the Cunard Line without a struggle; instead, both companies made efforts to attract customers by other means.

In 1911 the White Star Line commissioned the first of three 45,000-ton ships of the *Olympic* class, which offered unsurpassed levels of comfort and luxury, albeit at a moderate speed of 21 knots. The second ship of this class was the *Titanic* of 1912,

The Cunard express liners *Lusitania* and *Mauretania* of 1907, and the three White Star liners of the *Olympic* class which had entered service in 1911, required a response from the Hamburg-America Line, and Albert Ballin met the challenge by commissioning the three ships of the *Imperator* class starting in 1913. At more than 50,000grt these ships were the largest in the world, but they were not designed to compete for the Blue Riband, even though their service speed of just on 24 knots came close to that of the two Cunard ships. The *Vaterland,* shown here, built by Blohm + Voss in Hamburg and delivered to Hapag in 1914, was requisitioned in 1917 while in the USA, and entered service there as the *Leviathan.* In June 1923 on trials for the United States Lines, with the gulf stream behind her, she recorded a continuous speed of 27.48 knots for a period of 25 hours.* In 1914, during trials for the Hapag company, the ship had managed 25.84 knots when running at her maximum power of 90,700shp.

whose maiden voyage ended famously in tragedy. It is still claimed right to the present day that the intention was for the *Titanic* to win the Blue Riband on this crossing, but the facts contradict this.

The Hamburg-America line responded by building the three luxurious 50,000-tonners of the *Imperator* class; these vessels came into service from 1913, and offered a service speed of 23.5 knots.

The company from which Cunard had just taken the Blue Riband, NDL, was unable to trump her own four-funnel liners, for its financial position at the time made any response impossible.

It was more than twenty years before the contest for the Blue Riband was resumed, and this period was longer than any previous interval. The interruption, of course, was caused by the First World War. It is unlikely that anybody would have been able to predict that NDL would resume the battle.

*Braynard, Frank O, *World's Greatest Ship. The Story of the Leviathan,* (New York 1974) vol 2, p278

Prelude to the Last Round
North German Lloyd, 1929 to 1933

❖❖❖

BY THE Treaty of Versaille in June 1919 the victorious powers very thoroughly disposed of the maritime competition from the German Empire. The Germans had once claimed the world's second largest merchant fleet, but it was now reduced to practically nothing more than coastal ships. The Reich considered itself unable to provide compensation to the shipping companies, and as a result the reconstruction of the German merchant marine was fraught with problems. However, in 1921 North German Lloyd signed an agreement with the British, securing them the right to complete a steam ship currently under construction at a Danzig yard. When this 30,000grt liner entered service as the *Columbus* in 1924, her top speed of 19 knots made her no candidate for the Blue Riband, but it probably helped to show that the legendary Lloyd service was still able to attract passengers as it had in the past. In fact, the *Columbus* was so successful that the company was soon considering the construction of a slightly faster sister ship.

By 1926 Lloyd was already contemplating what was known as a five-day ship, a liner which would be able to complete the crossing from the English Channel to New York in five days. This would require a speed of 26 knots, which in turn called for a ship of at least 46,000grt. Around this time American compensation was received for the Lloyd ships requisitioned in the USA in 1917, giving Director Glässel the chance to persuade his board colleagues to take an even larger step: to place contracts immediately for two 46,000grt steamers with a service speed of 26.25 knots.

In December 1926 the construction contracts were signed with Blohm + Voss in Hamburg and AG Weser in Bremen. A full twenty years had passed since the previous generation of fast ocean liners had been designed, and in that period marine tech-

Promotional postcard for the *Bremen*.

nology had made enormous advances – not least due to the war. Reliable reduction gearboxes had now been developed which allowed physically smaller turbines to work at better efficiency and the boilers on these ships could now generate a steam pressure of up to 23at. It was clear that these new liners would satisfy the highest of expectations. They were launched on successive days in August 1928, christened with the names *Europa* and *Bremen*, and for the first time the world could admire their innovative streamlined design with their rounded foreship and impressive bow bulge. Both ships were due to commence trials

in the spring of 1929, but this was postponed by several months due to a strike by dockyard workers. To make matters even worse, the *Europa* went up in flames in March 1929 at the fitting out pier, and sank to the bottom. It was feared that the ship was a total loss, but although the decks were damaged by the fire, it proved possible to rebuild them, although the work took several months.

In July 1929 the *Bremen* set off on her maiden voyage, and, as expected, she celebrated by winning the Blue Riband. The previous record of 26.06 knots had been set by the *Mauretania* in 1909, but the *Bremen* was able to push this up to 27.83 knots. In March 1930, the *Europa* also proved her outstanding qualities, and with a speed of 27.91 knots she obliged her sister ship to relinquish the Blue Riband. Right from the start both ships proved highly popular with the international travelling public, as the following figures show. In 1928 NDL could claim 8.72 per cent of the total North Atlantic passenger traffic, but in 1929 this rose to 9.78 per cent and in 1930 to 14.47 per cent. The *Bremen* had come into service in July 1929, followed by the *Europa* in March 1930. In 1931, the first full year for both ships, Lloyd's proportion of the traffic rose to 17.16 per cent, and in 1932 the figure rose to no less than 18.18 per cent. After this the proportion diminished slightly due to the steady advent of new vessels from the shipping lines of other countries. Incidentally, these percentage figures merely provide evidence of the proportion of transatlantic passengers carried by Lloyd's express steamers; they tell us nothing about the ships' economic success. The total numbers of passengers for each year had fallen from 1,060,747 in 1928 to only 642,709 in the year 1932.[*]

At this point we need to bear in mind the economic background of international travel which impinged so severely on the years 1926 to 1932. This is important as it counters the repeated claims[**] that the *Bremen* and *Europa* were built with state

[*] Kludas, Arnold, 'Die deutschen Schnelldampfer', in *Deutsches Schiffahrtsarchiv*, vol 11 1988, pp177-214

[**] For example, Napier, Rob, 'The North German Lloyd and Bremen' (IV), 1929, in *Nautical Research Journal*, No. 4, (Bethesda 1985), p171; Miller, William H, *The Great Luxury Liners 1927-1954*, (New York 1981), p37, and in Eliseo, Maurizio, *REX*, (Parma 1992), p30

Streamlining in ship design: the *Europa* on the stocks at Blohm + Voss in Hamburg (left), and the *Bremen* at the Columbus quay in Bremerhaven.

The *Bremen* under the framework of the stocks of the AG Weser shipyard belonging to the Deschimag company.

In 1926 Managing Director Ernst Glässel initiated the project to build the Lloyd express steamers *Bremen* and *Europa*.

support which was not the case. North German Lloyd had the ships built on its own account. When the company ordered the two ships in December 1926, it was basing its calculations on promising conditions and firm hopes of success. The conditions eventually altered drastically as follows.

First, the estimated cost of each ship was 48 million Reichsmarks, but in fact the final cost was 68 million marks. Second, in 1925 the government of the USA agreed to pay compensation to the German shipping companies for the ships which had been requisitioned in US ports in 1917. The Lloyd company was assigned $27,240,000, around 100 million Reichsmarks. This money would have secured the repayment of the credits which

the firm had set up for the construction of the new ships. Then, from October 1929 to 1933 the greatest economic crisis in world history affected international shipping very severely, and shipping company results were hit extremely badly. This crisis led to the formation of the Hapag-Lloyd Union in March 1930; this was a de facto consolidation on the part of both shipping companies, since all income and expenses had to be divided in half. In July 1930 NDL received the first payment of compensation from the USA of $7.34 million.

By this date Germany was no longer able to pay the war reparations to which she was obliged. The Young plan of 1930, which regulated the payments, was superseded in 1932 by the

The *Bremen* with her low funnels; in 1930 they had to be extended to improve smoke dispersion.

Profile of the *Bremen* of 1929 with the original low funnels. In the summer of 1930 the *Bremen* and *Europa* were fitted with funnel caps five metres high; see profile of *Europa*.

TS *Bremen*

Owner: North German Lloyd, Bremen.

Builder: Deschimag, AG Weser, Bremen; Yard No. 872.

Specification: 51,656grt / 14,565dwt / 938.6ft overall length / 101.7ft beam / four sets geared turbines; Weser / 105,000shp / four screws / 26.3 knots / 811 first-class, 500 second-class, 300 tourist class, 617 third-class passengers / crew 966.

Career: 16.8.1928 launched / 16.7.1929 maiden voyage Bremerhaven–New York, winning the Blue Riband at 27.83 knots average speed / also set new record on return crossing with 27.91 knots / 6.1933 improved record speed to 28.51 knots on the Ambrose–Cherbourg route / 30.8.1939 steamed from New York to Murmansk without passengers due to threat of war / 10.12.1939 from Murmansk to Bremerhaven / 1940 naval barrack ship in Bremerhaven / planned transport for intended invasion of Great Britain / 16.-18.3.1941 completely burned out in Bremerhaven after deliberately being set on fire/by 1946 broken up / 1.4.1946 final remains of double bottom towed up the Weser, stranded opposite Nordenham, where they can still be seen today when the tide is very low.

Hoover moratorium, and then by the annulment of the Young plan the same year. These negotiations had dire consequences for the shipping companies, as the compensation payments were balanced against the Reich's debts. The Reich could claim a foreign affairs success, but Lloyd suffered to the tune of 80 million Reichsmarks, on which all the company's plans were based; incidentally, Hapag suffered even worse.

By 1932 Hapag and Lloyd required bridging credits due to inadequate income, and these were secured by the Reich. From this point on the fortunes of Hapag and Lloyd hung in the bal-ance. Until the start of the Second World War and even later, the Reich and the major banks determined the future of the Hapag-Lloyd union by the power of their financial holdings.

From this chronological account it is clear how Lloyd built its latest express steamers without benefit of subsidy, and that this was in every respect a reasonable business decision. It was only when the depression occurred that the shipping company's critical situation developed.

Another question often raised is whether North German Lloyd might not have been able to foresee that its new vessels

Profile of the *Europa* in 1930.

TS *Europa*

Owner: North German Lloyd, Bremen.

Builder: Blohm + Voss, Hamburg; Yard No. 479.

Specification: 49,746grt / 12,840dwt / 936.7ft overall length / 101.7ft beam / four sets geared turbines; Blohm + Voss / 105,000shp / four screws / 26.3 knots / 860 first-class, 500 second-class, 305 tourist-class, 617 third-class passengers / crew 965.

Career: 15.8.1928 launched / 26.3.1929 fire broke out when ship was almost completed; commissioning of *Europa* delayed by several months / 19.3.1930 maiden voyage Bremerhaven – New York; *Europa* relieved sister ship *Bremen* of Blue Riband at 27.91 knots / 27.6 to 2.7.1933 new record crossing from Cherbourg to Ambrose: 27.93 knots / 29.1.1937 rescued three shipwrecked sailors from German tanker *Olifer* / 10.1939 navy barrack ship in Bremerhaven / planned transport for intended invasion of England / 1942 planned refit as aircraft carrier / 5.1945 US prize of war / 25.8.1945 commissioned as US troop transport AP 177 / 8.6.1946 transferred to France; renamed *Liberté*, Cie Gén Transatlantique, Le Havre / 8.12.1946 driven against wreck of *Paris* in Le Havre in storm; sunk on even keel / 15.4.1947 raised / 9.11.1947 towed to St Nazaire, there repaired and renovated / 18.10.1949 fire damaged 80 cabins / 17.8.1950 first voyage Le Havre – New York for the C.G.T ./ 16.11.1961 laid up in Le Havre / 30.1.1962 to La Spezia, broken up by Terrestre Marittima.

would force the hand of its rival shipping companies, and that this development would, in fact, reduce the market share of the German liners after 1932. As in the period before 1914, a gigantic maritime contest very soon broke out. This was certainly predictable, but the Germans had hoped that it would not occur in the form which it eventually took. Carl Stimming was a privy councillor as well as President of NDL, and at a press conference in Hamburg, held to mark the imminent trials of the *Europa*, he stated that his company naturally acknowledged the right of all its rivals to follow the course marked out by the new liners, and to overtake Lloyd if they could. What would be regrettable, however, would be the total distortion of the competitive situation which would result if public means were employed in the construction and running of such ships.[°] Stimming's warning turned out to be justified. After 1931 overall passenger totals on the North Atlantic routes declined drastically. The French parliament debated long and hard whether to proceed with the construction of the great French liner–

[°]*Schiffbau* , No 5, (Berlin 1930), p100

115

Rudolf Blohm at the launch of the *Europa*. Blohm was head of the Hamburg dockyard Blohm + Voss, whose engineers were responsible for the advanced overall design of the two Lloyd fast steamers.

The *Europa* after a period in dock on the lower Elbe.

whether the project was sensible, and whether it was responsible to use state funds to support it. In January 1932 the *Bremer Weserzeitung* (Bremen Weser Journal) printed a comprehensive report of the matter, giving special emphasis to the French Marine Minister's claim that it had, of course, been Germany which had started this trend by granting state support to its shipping companies. Managing Director Glässel refuted these accusations, and explained that Germany had been forced to build new ships because its merchant fleet had been relinquished to other countries, whereas the same reason could not be valid for other states. This line of argument undoubtedly struck the core of the problem, but it did nothing to eliminate it.

Opposite page: the *Europa* at full speed in heavy weather.

Italia ante Portas
The Italian Liner, 1933 to 1935

◆◆◆

The Italia liner *Rex* in New York.

THE HISTORY of Italian passenger steam navigation started in the nineteenth century, but Italian liners did not play a significant role until the start of the twentieth century. After the First World War the country's shipping companies and shipbuilding industry made equally impressive progress, and both were promoted by the state – especially after Mussolini took over the government.

In the 1920s the leading Italian shipping companies in the North Atlantic service were Navigazione Generale Italiana, generally abbreviated to NGI, which was the result of an amalgamation in 1881, and Lloyd Sabaudo, founded in 1907; both compa-

nies were based in Genoa. The directors of these two concerns followed with great interest the building of the *Bremen* and *Europa* in Germany, and responded by drawing up their own plans with the encouragement of the Italian government. In the summer of 1928 the state created the Istituto di Credito Italiano, whose task was to secure the financing of major shipbuilding projects. The directors of the shipping companies, accompanied by representatives of the Istituto, inspected the *Bremen*, and it was agreed that both the rival companies would build a fast steamer based on the German vessels, with the intention of operating the ships as part of a common service.

In December 1929 NGI granted the contracts for the liners to the Ansaldo yard in Genoa, while Lloyd Sabaudo ordered its ship from Cantieri Riuniti dell' Adriatico, based in Monfalcone, near

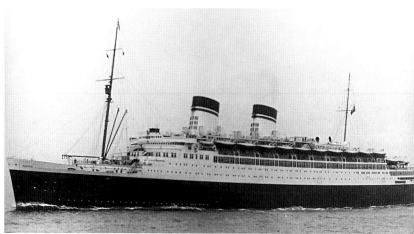

The *Conte di Savoia* of 48,502grt was built in Trieste in 1932, and only just failed to win the Blue Riband. Externally, the ship was more modern and elegant in appearance than the *Rex* with her somewhat disjointed superstructure.

The *Rex* in September 1932 on her mile run – the speed proving course – in the Gulf of Genoa.

Profile of the *Rex* of 1932.

TS *Rex*

Owner: 'Italia' Flotta Riunite Cosulich, Lloyd Sabaudo e Navigazione Generale, Genoa.

Builder: G Ansaldo & Co, Sestri Ponente, Genoa; Yard No 296.

Specification: 51,062grt / 12,448dwt / 880ft overall length / 97ft beam / four sets geared turbines / 100,000shp / four screws / 27.5 knots / 604 first-class, 378 second-class, 410 tourist-class, 866 third-class passengers / crew 756.

Career: 1.8.1931 launched, intended originally as *Guglielmo Marconi*, for Navigazione Generale Italiana / 27.9.1932 maiden voyage Genoa–Naples–Gibraltar– New York / 1. to 16.8.1933 won Blue Riband at 28.92 knots / 5.1940 North Atlantic service halted / 6.1940 laid up in Pola / 5.9.1943 transferred to Capodistria, Trieste / 8.9.1943 set on fire by rockets from British aircraft / 9.9.1943 sank in shallow water after renewed rocket attack by British / after 1947: broken up by Yugoslavian salvage teams in situ.

Trieste. The ships were to due to be completed in the summer of 1932. These orders coincided with the initial phase of the great world shipping crisis which has already been mentioned, and the situation soon turned out to be much worse than originally feared. In 1930 consideration was given to cancelling the new vessels, but the Fascist government was unwilling to abandon the scheme. A solution was found by merging Navigazione Generale Italiana with Lloyd Sabaudo (together with the Cosulich Line, which Lloyd also controlled). The merger took effect on 2 January 1932, forming the 'Italia' Flotta Riunite Cosulich-Lloyd Sabaudo-NGI, Genoa. The majority holding of the 'Italia' line was held by the Italian state.

The *Rex* and *Conte di Savoia* were launched in 1931, at that time still the property of Navigazione Generale Italiana and

The launch of the *Rex* on 1 August 1931.

Lloyd Sabaudo respectively. However, by the time of their completion in the autumn of 1932 they already bore the impressive funnel markings of the new 'Italia' concern. Only slightly delayed, both ships entered service in 1932; the *Rex* in September and the *Conte di Savoia* in November. Until then it had been assumed that the vessels were identical sister ships, but now the public became aware that this was by no means the case. The many major and minor differences are evident just by perusing the photographs, although the two essential differences are not readily apparent; the *Conte di Savoia* was 65ft shorter, and her engines were around ten per cent less powerful than those of the *Rex*.

With the winter season imminent, no record attempts were planned initially. Captain Tarabotto was then authorised to carry out a record attempt for the year 1933, but he was left to determine the date himself. He chose August, and his attempt was successful. At 28.82 knots the *Rex* was exactly one knot faster than the *Europa*, and she duly claimed the Blue Riband for Italy. Before this attempt many interested parties had debated whether a record crossing over the southern route from Gibraltar to New York should be recognised as valid for the Blue Riband. However, there were no serious objections, since it was hardly reasonable to demand that the Italians should steam from Cherbourg solely for the purpose of a record attempt. And even if anyone had harboured objections, the difference of a full knot

The *Rex* steaming out on her maiden voyage Genoa–New York on 27 September 1932.

was convincing, and made further debate superfluous. The *Rex* did not make a record attempt in the opposite direction. The *Conte di Savoia* made an attempt at wresting the Blue Riband from the *Rex*, but she was unsuccessful, even though her final speed was only 0.2 knots slower.

Incidentally, as mentioned earlier, the Hales Trophy had been donated in 1935, and at that time the *Rex* became the first ship to be awarded the trophy as an external symbol of her triumph. However, back in August 1933 the crew celebrated in their own manner by hoisting a 95ft (29m) long pennant-shaped blue riband to the mainmast, each metre symbolising one knot of the overall speed that the ship had achieved.

121

Ruban Bleu for France

The Cie Gén Transatlantique, 1935 to 1938

♦♦♦

This wonderful portrait of a grandiose liner was the work of the French maritime painter Marin-Marie; it is a gouache of the *Normandie* in the port of New York.

FRANCE'S GREAT transatlantic shipping company, the Compagnie Générale Transatlantique, was originally known as the Cie Générale Maritime, but was renamed in 1864. The company's name was abbreviated to CGT, and in later years it was usually known internationally simply as the French Line. Right from the outset the concern was highly subsidised and therefore subject to changes in government thinking. Until the start of the twentieth century the shipbuilding policy of the CGT was aimed at keeping abreast of its direct rivals, primarily the two German shipping companies Hapag and Lloyd, since these were the two concerns which also used the Channel route for Atlantic crossings to New York. In the period before 1914 the French began to aim somewhat higher, a good example is the 23,666grt steamer *France*. This vessel came into service in 1912, and her service speed of 24 knots was only surpassed by the *Mauretania* and *Lusitania* at that time. In 1927, nine years after the end of the First World War, the CGT commissioned a modern super-liner in the shape of the 43,000 ton *Ile de France*, although this ship was never intended to compete for the Blue Riband.

Eventually the CGT drew up plans for a super-liner, and this project was under way before the two Lloyd liners were commissioned. The work was carried out by CGT in collaboration with the domestic yard Chantiers et Ateliers de St Nazaire Penhoët. The brilliant Russian-born shipbuilder Wladimir Yourkewitsch, adopted the new ideas of the Germans – especially the bulbous bow, the flared stem formed of plates, instead of the former straight stem of cast iron, and streamlined shape, although he refined these features considerably. His contract stated that the new vessel had to improve on the performance of the German ships, and Yourkewitsch embraced this challenge with real determination. There were to be no financial limitations for the new liner, as it was viewed as an object of national prestige; however, the ship was to be as economic as possible to operate, and these conditions provided a double motivation for all the personnel involved. Then, in May 1930, came the news that the Cunard Line intended to build a gigantic ship in response to the German challenge.

From this moment it was clear that France, the Cie Générale Transatlantique and the Chantiers et Ateliers de St Nazaire could not allow their vessel to be inferior to this new ship; it had to offer at least equal performance. To build the new liner the CGT had been granted a loan of 120.5 million francs over a period of 20 years at 5.5 per cent interest. The state would act as guarantor for the interest, and the contract also stated that an annual subsidy of 50 to 150 million francs would be paid to the shipping company starting in July 1933.

By 1929 the construction of new stocks had begun in St Nazaire, and the length of the structure gave a first intimation of the gigantic size of the ship which was to be built here. On 26 January 1931 the first plate was laid, and the keel of the later *Normandie* began to take shape. When the ship was launched in October 1932 the red-leaded hull gave a formidable impression of the majestic size of this new vessel. The occasion of this festive event was also used to provide the public with a few facts and figures: the new ship's size was to be almost 80,000grt, surpassing that of the German liners by a good 50 per cent. She was the world's first ship with a length of more than 1,000ft. In contrast, the number of passengers was 10 per cent less than the capacity of the German liners, whereas the crew was to be 30 per cent larger – these figures implied an improvement in terms of service and luxury which was almost unimaginable. The speed required to gain the Blue Riband was to be achieved with the help of a turbo-electric propulsion system, whereby the ship's turbines powered generators which in turn supplied electrical current for the drive motors. This was a relatively new method of propulsion, and was being used for the first time in a fast liner. One German expert described the *Normandie* with these words: 'the French ship incorporates a greater wealth of advanced creative thinking than has ever been seen before; the hull form

The *Normandie* during a landing manoeuvre in New York.

exploits all the experience that has been gained with bulged bow ships in contrary seas, and represents a sensible combination of well-shaped upper foreship, clipper bow, and enclosed turtle-deck.'°

It took two and a half years to equip the *Normandie* and install the internal fittings. This long length of time was due primarily to the major shipping crisis which has already been mentioned several times, rather than the many innovations which the ship incorporated. There had been no interruptions in the construction of the liner, but the speed of progress was evidently slowed down, in the hope that the ship might benefit from a period of rising economic confidence. Trials were held in the spring of 1935, and the expected superior speed was achieved in full; the *Normandie* steamed at 31 knots for a period of several hours. This much had been expected, but what was quite astonishing was the fact that the steamer hardly consumed more fuel at her service speed of 29 knots than the *Ile de France* did at hers of 23.5 knots – and this for a vessel twice the size. Of this Wladimir Yourkewitsch could justifiably be proud.

On 29 May 1935 the world's largest and fastest ship set off on her maiden voyage on the route Le Havre–Southampton–New York. Of course, at this time the Italian *Rex* was still officially the fastest ship, but the whole world assumed that Captain Pugnet would gain the Blue Riband with his new liner. When the crossing was completed, the *Normandie* had proved to be more than one knot faster than the *Rex*,

and the reception in New York for the new holder of the Blue Riband was tumultuous. The crew of the French liner had prepared a long 'ruban bleu', following the pattern of the *Rex*, and hoisted it proudly once the victory was theirs. The *Normandie* was also successful on the return voyage, when she relieved the *Bremen* of the record which she had held for six years. The *Normandie* also set one more 'record' of which the designers were not quite so proud: she suffered from high-speed vibration, and became the new holder of the title 'cocktail shaker' which the *Deutschland* had held thirty-five years earlier. However, whereas Hapag never managed to solve the earlier liner's problem, the *Normandie* was eventually fitted with new four-bladed propellers to replace the earlier three-bladed ones, and this effectively eliminated the annoying vibration.

The brilliant Russian-born Wladimir Yourkewitsch, who was responsible for the design of the *Normandie* .

The *Normandie* at maximum speed on trials.

°Dr Ing E Foerster in *Werft – Reederei – Hafen*, issue 10, 1936, p157

Profile of the *Normandie* in 1935.

In the meantime the Cunard Line's rival ship was taking shape in England in the form of the *Queen Mary*. Since passenger numbers were now declining constantly, the two shipping companies had agreed on a policy of peaceful co-existence, by which the two ships would share a common schedule. However, this would only apply once the *Queen Mary* had been commissioned in 1936. This gave the French the opportunity to correct an apparent failing which they had detected in the magnitude of the *Normandie*. With her gross tonnage of 79,280grt all the calculations predicted that the ship would take second place to the *Queen*, in which case she would then no longer be the world's largest ship. This was apparently utterly unacceptable to the French, and in the winter of 1935/36 they sent the liner back to the yard for various modifications. These changes, including the installation of a second-class lounge on the aft promenade deck, increased the ship's tonnage to 82,799, and eventually to 83,423grt. Thus it was that in 1936, when the *Queen* won the Blue Riband, the *Normandie* could still at least claim to be the world's largest ship.

In 1937 the *Normandie* was fitted with a third set of propellers of further revised design, and this modification increased her maximum speed to the point where she was able to regain the Blue Riband at 30.58 knots. This proved to be her last record voyage. Two years later, in 1939, she set off on her final crossing to New York, where she met her sad fate in 1942.

ETS *Normandie*

Owner: Cie Générale Transatlantique, Le Havre.

Builder: Chantiers et Ateliers de St. Nazaire (Penhoët), St. Nazaire; Yard No. T6.

Specification: 79,280grt / 12,000dwt / 1,029ft overall length / 118ft beam / four turbine sets, four generators, four electric drive motors; Alsthom / 130,000shp / four screws / 29 knots / 848 first-class, 670 second-class, 454 third-class passengers / crew 1345.

Career: 29.10.1932 launched. Initially planned as *President Paul Doumer* / 29.5.1935 maiden voyage Le Havre–Southampton–New York, won Blue Riband at 29.98 knots, 1937 further improved to 30.58 knots / record crossings also in opposite direction / 1936 refit: 82,799grt, later 83,423grt / 28.8.1939 laid up in New York due to threat of war / 12.12.1941 requisitioned by US Maritime Commission / 24.12.1941 to US Navy as *Lafayette* / 27.12.1941 to CGT Hudson Pier in New York, refit begun as US Navy Transport / 9.2.1942 cutting torch work on the promenade deck started a fire which quickly spread / 10.2.1942 barrels of part-frozen fire-fighting water stowed on the top deck made the *Lafayette* top-heavy, ship capsized / 7.8.1943 superstructure broken up and removed down to promenade deck; allowed ship to be righted / 13.9.1942 hull floated after pumping out internal water / planned refit as aircraft transport ship, not implemented / 11.10.1945 cancelled from list of US warships / 3.10.1946 sold for breaking up / towed to Pork Newark, broken up by Lipsett Inc.

The dining hall of the *Normandie* was designed to accommodate seven-hundred persons, and still ranks as one of the greatest testimonies to the art of internal architecture on passenger ships, and not just because of its immense dimensions: 305ft long, 46ft width, and 33ft high.

The Finale of a Contest
Cunard White Star, 1938 to 1952

Sir Percy Bates was Chairman of Cunard, and Chairman of the merged Cunard White Star line. He ensured that his company maintained the same pre-eminent position in the final phase of the contest for the Blue Riband that it had done at the start of its history a century previously.

FROM THE outset it was predictable that the success of the German ships would provoke the Cunard Line into joining in the renewed fray for the Blue Riband. Indeed, the company began its preparations back in 1927, when the German ships were laid down. The fact that two new nations – Italy and France – then joined the battle, neither of which had previously taken part in the Blue Riband competition, was another important reason for the British to fly the flag again so soon and impressively. When the plans for the *Normandie* became known, that was just the last push that Cunard needed. In May 1930 the company announced that a contract had been granted to the John Brown shipyard in Clydebank for the building of a 'giant liner'. Just a few months later, in December 1930, the keel had already been laid, one month before the French began work on the *Normandie*. However, on 10 December 1931 Cunard was forced to announce that work on the new vessel, No. 534, was to be halted until further notice. This news came as a horrible blow to the British public, but the truth was clear: the great international shipping crisis had brought severe losses for Cunard as for all other shipping companies.

Almost two years were to drift by before a ray of sunshine showed on the horizon. The British government was now ready to make a £4.5 million loan available to the Cunard Line: £3 million for the new vessel and another £1.5 million for running costs. The government also announced that a further £5 million would be granted at a later date for the construction of a sister ship. However, there was an important condition attached to this financial aid: Cunard and the White Star Line would have to merge. The union was completed in February 1934, and the new shipping company was established as Cunard White Star Limited.

Construction work on the new vessel could now resume in Glasgow and on 26 September 1934 the ship was christened with the name *Queen Mary* and launched. Like the *Normandie*, the *Queen Mary* was more than 1,000ft long, measured 80,000grt and offered similar levels of luxury. The hull of the new Cunard White Star liner had solid classical proportions when compared with the futuristic *Normandie*, but the turbine installation was designed to be at least the equal of her French rival.

On 27 May 1936 the ship was ready, and began her maiden voyage from Southampton to New York via Cherbourg. However, anyone who was expecting a record crossing at the first attempt was doomed to disappointment. Captain Britten insisted on continuing with the Cunard tradition of taking his time to run in the engines of the new ship carefully. It was not until August of that year that Britten made his attempt to eclipse the *Normandie*, and his ship duly reached New York as the new winner of the Blue Riband. On the return crossing she also set a new record for the eastbound route. For the first time the mark for the Blue Riband now lay above 30 knots, as the *Queen* had achieved an average speed of 30.14 knots. Naturally, Mr Hales now wanted to present his trophy to the newly victorious ship, but to his immense consternation he learned that Cunard White Star had 'taken no part in any competition', but was simply carrying out scheduled voyages; the company was therefore unable to accept any trophy, he was told. Undoubtedly, the directors of Cunard White Star had realised that their refusal to accept the trophy would win greater publicity for them than would the Hales trophy itself.

Cunard White Star and the CGT had agreed to adopt a common schedule for their premier ships and the swapping of the Blue Riband between the *Queen Mary* and the *Normandie* has

The *Queen Mary* in 1936, entering New York as the new holder of the Blue Riband.

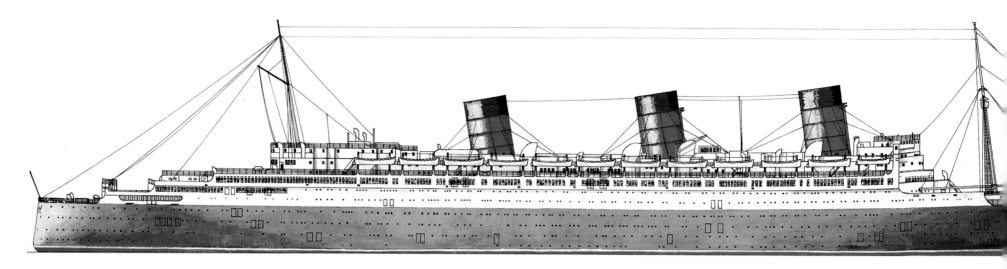

Profile of the *Queen Mary* in 1936.

The *Queen Elizabeth*, whose 83,673grt was not exceeded by any passenger ship in the world for a period of almost fifty years.

also been described already. With her record crossing in August 1938 the *Queen Mary* eventually pushed the record up to 30.99 knots.

That this record figure stood from that year right through to 1952 was due mainly to the Second World War which broke out in 1939. In other circumstances the *Queen Elizabeth* might also have entered the competition after 1940. This 83,000-tonner, belonging to Cunard White Star, had been launched in 1938 and entered service in 1940, but her first role was as a troop transport. It was not until October 1946 that the *Queen Elizabeth* made her first commercial voyage to New York, and at that time there were more important matters in people's minds than the Blue Riband.

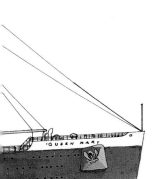

TS *Queen Mary*

Owner: Cunard White Star, Liverpool.

Builder: John Brown & Co, Clydebank; Yard No 534.

Specification: 80,774grt / 17,000dwt / 1,019.4ft overall length / 118.5ft beam / four sets geared turbines; dockyard / 158,000shp / four screws / 29 knots / 776 first-(cabin) class, 784 tourist-class, 579 third-class passengers / crew 1101.

Career: 27.12.1930 laid down / 10.12.1931 construction halted / 3.4.1934 work resumed / 26.9.1934 launched / 27.5.1936 maiden voyage Southampton–Cherbourg–New York / 20. to 24.8.1936 won Blue Riband at 30.14 knots; improved to 30.99 knots in 1938 / records also set in easterly direction / 1937: measured 81,235grt / 9.1939 laid up in New York / 1.3.1940 commissioned as troop transport ship / 2.10.1942 USA-Clyde crossing: cruiser HMS *Curacoa* crossed *Queen Mary*'s bows 20 nautical miles Northwest of Bloody Foreland (Ireland) during U-boat alarm which later turned out to be false. Warship cut in two, sank with 338 men; only 26 rescued / 9.1946 to the dockyard for overhaul and refit as passenger ship. 81,237grt, 711 first-class, 707 cabin-class, 577 tourist-class passengers / 31.7.1947 first post-war crossing Southampton–New York / 18.8.1967 sold to town of Long Beach / 31.10.1967 final departure from Southampton, en route for Long Beach / 10.5.1971 opened in Long Beach as hotel, museum and conference centre / 1988 to Disney Corporation.

A contrast between two historical periods at the fitting-out quay in Clydebank: 1hp in the foreground, 200,000hp in the hull of the *Queen Mary* in the background.

Steaming across the Atlantic at 35 knots: an aerial photograph of the *United States*.

The End of an Era
The United States, 1952

◆◆◆

EXACTLY ONE hundred years after Edward K Collins conducted the American interlude in the competition for the Blue Riband, the USA returned to the stage to give a powerful closing chord. On 8 February 1950, in Newport News, Virginia, the keel was laid for a new vessel which at the time was shrouded in secrecy. Gibbs & Co, the most famous American naval architects, were responsible for the ship's design, the contract having been awarded by the United States Lines Company of New Jersey, and the vessel was built at the Newport News Shipbuilding & Dry Dock Company. The shipyard's motto stood in gold letters on its administration building: 'We will always build good ships, at a profit if we can, at a loss if we must – but always good ships'; these sentiments caused great anticipation of the outcome of the project.

The United States Lines (USL) had been founded in 1921 as successor to the United States Mail Steamship Company. Its task was to administer the many passenger ships belonging to the United States Shipping Board (USSB), which primarily consisted of the former Hapag and Lloyd liners requisitioned in 1917, together with the large series of standard passenger ships which had been built in the First World War. Although a private concern, the company was dependent to a very great extent on the US government, for it only provided administration for these ships; they remained the property of the USSB. In the 1920s the USL owned the largest ship in the world in the shape of the *Leviathan*, formerly the Hapag company's *Vaterland*, and in 1932/33 two new 30,000-ton vessels were commissioned for the New York–Hamburg service. These were the *Manhattan* and the *Washington*, and in 1940 they were joined by the 34,000grt *America*.

The First World War had transformed the United States into the world's leading maritime nation by a considerable margin – at least in terms of tonnage – and by the end of the Second World War the nation was also the planet's leading superpower. With this global status in mind, it was only natural that the new vessel

The *United States* enters Bremerhaven in the early morning.

133

from Newport News should be designed to reflect the new splendour of the USA; indeed, not only the splendour, but also the military might. In fact, this ship was designed not only to win and hold the Blue Riband in times of peace, but also to act as a powerful, fast method of transporting 14,000 troops to the overseas location of any future war. The vessel was therefore viewed as a military secret, and the US Navy incorporated in her its considerable experience in transporting personnel and goods. The military nature of the enterprise also explains the fact that this ship was the first of its type to be built in a dry dock, largely con-

cealed from the eyes of the curious, instead of on conventional stocks. To the Pentagon this troop transport was worth $45 million, so that is the amount it contributed to the overall construction price of $77 million.

On 23 June 1951 the ship was named *United States* in a solemn ceremony. Once launched, the dimensions of the mighty hull were exposed to the eyes of the world for the first time. She was 990ft long, with a

A view into the central area of the first-class dining room on the *United States*.

Profile of the *United States*.

The second-class drawing room
on the *United States*.

beam of 101ft. Experts all over the globe got out their slide-rules and raised their eyebrows in surprise, as a ship of these dimensions must surely measure significantly more than the stated figure of 53,300grt. According to European methods of calculation, the *United States*'s must have been more than 60,000grt, even though it was known that US figures for ship measurement were always 15 to 20 per cent below the equivalent European figures. It is also no secret that the American methods of calculation allowed for considerable manipulations. The *United States* is actually a good example of this, for, without any external changes being made, her stated tonnage diminished several times, and in 1967 had fallen to only 38,216grt. The speed achieved on trials in June 1952 remained a state secret for many years, as did the power of the engines required to achieve it. It was only in 1968 that the world discovered that the engines developed 240,000shp, giving the vessel a maximum speed of 42 knots. However, these figures are also open to dispute; the law which states that the longer the hull, the faster the ship does not nullify the other relevant law, that, beyond a certain speed, engine power must be raised by the square in order to achieve one additional knot of speed.

Whatever the true figures, the world's public was satisfied by the results achieved on the ship's first two crossings. The maiden voyage, begun on 3 July 1953, took the ship from New York to Southampton, and the average speed of 35.59 knots left absolutely no room for doubt that the *United States* would win the Blue Riband on the return crossing. On 15 July 1953 the ship steamed into New York as flagship of the US merchant fleet, and was able also to savour a great triumph: she was the new holder of the Blue Riband with a speed of 34.51 knots, more than 3.5 knots faster than the *Queen Mary*, which had set a mark of 30.99 knots fourteen years previously.

When he completed his record run in 1953 Captain Manning brought the history of the Blue Riband contest to a close. Even before the Second World War passenger aircraft had shown that they would inevitably become a force to be reckoned with, but during the war the technology made such vast progress that regular transatlantic flights no longer presented any problems. When the *United States* was under construction it might have

Owner: United States Lines, New York.

Builder: Newport News Sb & D D Co, Newport News; Yard No 488.

Specification: 53,329grt / 13,016dwt / 990ft overall length / 101.6ft beam / four sets geared turbines; Westinghouse / 173,000shp / four screws / 31 knots / 871 first-class, 508 cabin-class, 549 tourist-class passengers / crew 1093.

Career: 23.6.1951 floated / 3.7.1952 maiden voyage New York–Southampton. The *United States* broke all North Atlantic speed records in both directions, winning the Blue Riband with 34.51 knots. The record still stands today / In the winter months the service was extended to Bremerhaven / 1961: 51,988grt / 1962: 44,893grt; 1967: tonnage reduced to 38,216 / 8.11.1969 laid up in Newport News, later in Hampton Roads / 2.1973 to US Maritime Administration. Laid up in Norfolk, Virginia / 1978 to United States Cruises, Seattle, which wanted to reactivate the vessel as a cruise ship, but was unable to pay the full cost / 4.3.1989 transferred to Newport News / 27.4.1992 to Marmara Marine Inc, New York, which belonged to the Turkish Sadikoglu / 4.6.1992 towed to Istanbul by the *Smit Rotterdam*, laid up in Tuzla. Refit planned as cruise ship / 1993 Panama became new home port / 1.11.1993 towed to Sebastopol, where asbestos insulation was removed / 15.5.1994 ship returned to Tuzla, where Sadikoglu shipyard began refit as cruise ship. However, this project suffered from financial difficulties from the outset, and did not progress beyond the removal of the old internal fittings / 25.7.1996 towed to Philadelphia naval dockyard by the *Smit New York*, laid up / 11.1996 to Edward Cantor; laid up again.

been possible to believe in a 50:50 share of the market between aircraft and ships, but by 1960 a new perspective gave a much more realistic outlook. Now it was only a question of time before jet aircraft would become the sole means of transport on overseas routes. It is true that the French, the Italians and the British commissioned new fast transatlantic liners in the 1960s, but by that time the Blue Riband was no longer their ambition. Finally,

in 1969, the first Boeing 747 jet rose into the sky, and in so doing relegated the North Atlantic passenger ships to history.

On 8 November 1969 the *United States* was laid up in Newport News after seventeen proud years in service. Ship lovers and romantics all over the world have since lived in hope that the famous ship might be granted a second life; she has now survived for more than thirty years.

Landing manoeuvre assisted by tugs off the Bremerhaven Columbus quay.

A contemporary portrait of the last holder of the Blue Riband, the *United States*, as painted by T C Skinner.

Adieu, Blue Riband – good luck to the *United States*.

The Super-Liners that Never Were

◆◆◆

THE URGE to improve technical performance and to surpass previous achievements is as old as the history of technology itself. As we have found throughout this book, this certainly applies to the speed of ships. At the beginning of the twentieth century the competition for the Blue Riband developed almost into a spectator event, giving the great maritime nations involved on the North Atlantic route the chance to display their abilities. Inevitably, a number of interesting fast steamer projects were planned which never came to fruition. Despite this it is appropriate to mention them briefly.°

In 1902 the young German engineer Johann Schütte designed a fast steam ship which was expected to exceed the speed of the *Kaiser Wilhelm II* by two knots, despite being only the same size and having the same engine power.°° In controlled experiments in tank testing Schütte had discovered that this could be achieved with a ship having a broad hull, a cruiser stern and a shallower draught than normal. For a while North German Lloyd considered adopting the idea, but eventually decided against it and ordered another of the proven four-funnel vessels instead, in the shape of the *Kronprinzessin Cecilie*. The increased speed of the Schütte liner would have been advantageous in terms of scheduling, but the advantage would only have applied to the new ship, and the overall effect on the standard schedules of the fast Lloyd steamers would have been negative. An additional factor in the mind of Lloyd directors would certainly have been the *Kaiser Friedrich* disaster, which would undoubtedly have led them to follow the guideline 'no more experiments'. In terms of the Blue Riband, the projected ship might have been able to surpass the Hapag and Lloyd four-funnel ships, and even compared with the *Lusitania* and *Mauretania*; her planned speed of 25.5 knots would have been truly remarkable.

In the period 1909 to 1914 John Pierpont Morgan pursued a

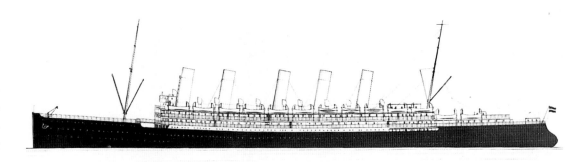

This drawing by Fritz G E Moll illustrates Johann Schütte's proposed design for a fast steamer.

plan to build two 55,000grt 30-knot steam ships, which were intended to enter service with the American Line of the International Mercantile Marine Company as the *Boston* and *Baltimore*. The renowned American shipbuilder William Francis Gibbs, together with his brother Frederic, were responsible for the plans. The four funnels were arranged in two pairs, as on the German steamers. The propulsion system was to be turbo-electric, which represented amazingly advanced thinking for the time, and they were to be fitted with oil-fired boilers. Although the project reached the stage of protracted towing experiments involving models, the planned vessel never made further progress. After the war a modified three-funnel version of the design was considered, this time with the support of the US Shipping Board, but in the 1920s the idea was quietly filed away again.

The next project was the product of Italian drawing boards in 1914. The Transatlantica Italiana company in Genoa, which was

---

° For detailed information on these projects see Williams, David L, and Richard P de Kerbrech, *Damned by Destiny* (Brighton 1982)
°° Kludas, Arnold, *Die Geschichte der deutschen Passagierschiffahrt* (Hamburg 1987) vol II, pp156, 167

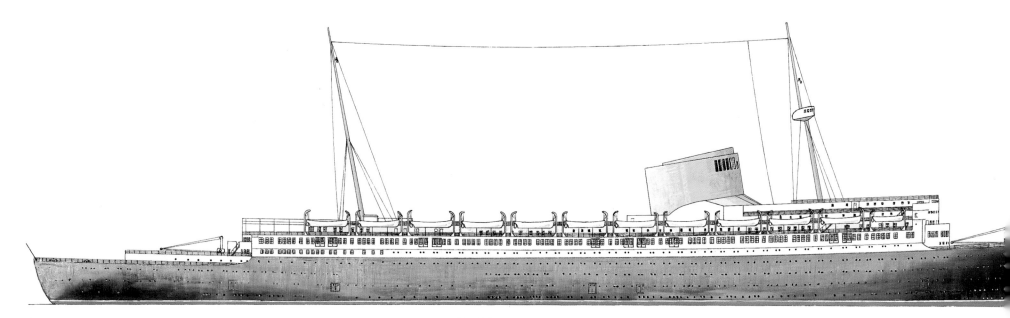

Profile of the proposed North German Lloyd *Viktoria*, drawn from the original shipyard plans.

virtually completely owned by the Hamburg-America Line, planned to build two 27,000grt steamers, whose nominal service speed of 25 knots lay close to the Blue Riband requirement. The two four-funnel ships were to be built at the Ansaldo shipyard, and even the vessels' names had already been decided: *Andrea Doria* and *Camillo di Cavour*. After the war the plans were abandoned.°

Two similar new vessels were planned in 1914 by the Italia Soc di Navigazione a Vapore which had been established with the help of the Hamburg-America Line, but the projects were not followed up.

In response to North German Lloyd's plans for fast steamers, the New York–London–Paris Steamship Company was established in New York in 1927. This concern was also known as the Blue Ribbon Line, and planned a transatlantic service employing six 35,000grt ships. The design speed of the liners was 33 to

35 knots, which anticipated the performance of the *United States*. The project, named *Flying Cloud*, had good financial backing, and by the early 1930s was already far advanced both technically and organisationally when the world economic crisis, and a failure to secure state support forced its abandonment. The two-funnel ships were even to feature a flight deck.

Success was also denied the American *Yankee-Clipper* project of 1937, although the gargantuan dimensions of the plan hardly makes this a surprise. The enterprise foresaw two 100,000-tonners for the United States Lines, each with two funnels and four screws, carrying 10,000 passengers in 5,000 cabins. The ships were to be powered by turbines rated at 380,000shp, or almost 500,000ihp, and their projected service speed was 34 to 38 knots. Around this time the US Maritime Commission was beginning to determine the course of US shipbuilding, and the Commission finally turned the project down.

In the period after 1937 the Bremen-based North German Lloyd company developed a plan in conjunction with Deschimag

---

°From a written statement by Maurizio Eliseo, Genoa.

for a new 80,000grt ship capable of 34 to 37 knots. The planning continued into the war years, and the National Socialist government expressed its support for the project; the ship was to have been completed as the *Viktoria* once the German victory was secured. By 1939 the design of the ship was finished, and every detail drawn, and extensive model experiments were successfully carried out in Hamburg. The outcome of the war finally put a stop to the plan.

In France in the late 1930s the Cie Générale Transatlantique was pushing ahead with its plans for a 100,000-tonner with a service speed of 34 knots, and so much progress had been made that the keel was due to be laid in St Nazaire in 1940, with a projected launch date in 1942. The maiden voyage of the two-funnel ship was planned for 1944. Yourkewitsch had drawn up the super-ship as a development of his own *Normandie* design, and its name was to be *Bretagne*. Once again the war intervened.

It is safe to say that none of these projected ships would have had a hope of being economically viable in operation, since there was already too much passenger capacity in the period after 1927, and the new vessels would just have added to the excess.

With these facts in mind, it is clear that the *Yankee Clipper*, *Viktoria* and *Bretagne* projects were purely objects of national aspiration, since they were not even devised until 1937. At that time the US government put a halt to the spending of taxes before it was too late; both Berlin and Paris preferred to wait until external forces decided the priorities for them.

The projects, 1902 to 1940

Shipping company Country	Year	grt	LOA (ft) Beam (ft)	Propulsion	ihp/shp Prop.	knot	Passengers, classes crew		
North German Lloyd Germany	1902	20700	688 89	2 quadruple-expansion steam engines	39000 i 2	25–26	750 I.,	300 II.,	900 III.
American Line USA	1909	55000	1000 106	Turbines, electric motors	185000 s 4	30	100 I.,	800 II., 1000	1200 III.
Trans. Italiana Italy	1914	27000	776 95	4 sets geared turbines	48000 s 4	25	420 I.,	338 II., 448	1594 III.
Blue Ribbon USA	1927	35000	900 90	4 sets geared turbines	160000 s 4	33–35	800 I.		
United States L. USA	1937	100000	1250 144	4 sets geared turbines	380000 s 4	34–38		10000 1750	
North German Lloyd Germany	1937	80000	1076 111	5 sets geared turbines	300000 s 5	34–37	400 I.,	700 II.,	900 III.
Cie. Gén. Trans. France	1938	100000	1148 138	Turbines, electric motors	320000 s 4	32		5000 I.	

An actual blue riband was very rarely hoisted after a ship broke the existing record, but the *Rex* did so in August 1933.

Epilogue

IN 1936 Sir Percy Bates wrote a letter to the London Times. At that time he was Chairman of the merged Cunard White Star Line, and his letter concerned the complex issue of international re-armament in the North Atlantic. His letter included the following words: 'Our chief competitors are really foreign governments and how far nationalism may be extended on the Atlantic to the complete disregard of economics it is impossible to say.'* Sir Percy was right. In the 1930s the free play of market forces in the North Atlantic, as promoted and practised by Albert Ballin, finally ceased to exist. In 1932 even the Germans had finally succumbed; Hapag and Lloyd were the last shipping companies to lose their unsubsidised virtue, when, at the height of the world economic crisis, they were obliged to ask the Reich government to guarantee bridging credit, without which neither of the companies would have been capable of staying in business.

The last round in the contest for the Blue Riband, which North German Lloyd had initiated in the 1920s, also proved to be the last round for international passenger shipping on the North Atlantic route. It was without doubt a wonderful period, and the grandiose Blue Riband liners of this final era–*Bremen*, *Europa*, *Rex*, *Normandie*, *Queen Mary* and *United States* have for many years been synonymous with the highest levels of creative, technical achievement. They also symbolise a culture of travelling which has disappeared; a manner of living which the aeroplane and the cruise ship cannot match, despite the fact that levels of luxury have now risen to even greater heights.

In 1840 the subsidies granted were precious and essential, but a hundred years later they came to represent significant amounts of taxpayers' money, some said too much, but perhaps we should not be too quick to frown upon such things. The taxpayers of today are used to very different demands on their money and perhaps they might be pleased if their governments, were to offer them so splendid and peaceful a return for their money, as the contest for the Blue Riband turned out to be.

---

*From a written statement by David Ramsay, Indian Wells.

Appendices

The Blue Riband† – record voyages in the westerly direction, 1838 to 1952

Period		Ship's name	Shipping company	Nation	From	To	Nautical miles	Days Hours Min.	knots
1838	4 Apr. – 22 Apr.	SIRIUS	Brit. & Am.	British	Queenstown	Sandy Hook	3583	18. 14. 22	8,03
1838	8 Apr. – 23 Apr.	GREAT WESTERN	Great West.	”	Avonmouth	New York	3220	15. 12. 00	8,66
1838	2 Jun – 17 Jun	GREAT WESTERN	”	”	”	”	3140	14. 16. 00	8,92
1839	18 May – 31 May	GREAT WESTERN	”	”	”	”	3086	13. 12. 00	9,52
1841	4 Jun – 15 Jun	COLUMBIA	Cunard	”	Liverpool	Halifax	2534	10. 19. 00	9,78 °
1843	29 Apr – 11 May	GREAT WESTERN	Great West.	”	”	New York	3068	12. 18. 00	10,03
1845	19 Jul – 29 Jul	CAMBRIA	Cunard	”	”	Halifax	2534	9. 20. 30	10,71 °
1848	3 Jun – 12 Jun	AMERICA	”	”	”	”	2534	9. 00. 16	11,71 °
1848	14 Oct – 23 Oct	EUROPA	”	”	”	”	2534	8. 23. 00	11,79 °
1850	18 May – 27 May	ASIA	”	”	”	”	2534	8. 14. 50	12,25 °
1850	11 Sep – 21 Sep	PACIFIC	Collins	U.S.A.	”	New York	3050	10. 04. 45	12,46 °
1851	6 Aug – 16 Aug	BALTIC	”	”	”	”	3039	9. 19. 26	12,91
1854	28 Jun – 7 Jul	BALTIC	”	”	”	”	3037	9. 16. 52	13,04
1856	19 Apr – 29 Apr	PERSIA	Cunard	British	”	Sandy Hook	3045	9. 16. 16	13,11 °
1863	19 Jul – 27 Jul	SCOTIA	”	”	Queenstown	New York	2820	8. 03. 00	14,46 °
1872	17 May – 25 May	ADRIATIC	White Star	”	”	Sandy Hook	2778	7. 23. 17	14,53
1875	30 Jul – 7 Aug	GERMANIC	”	”	”	”	2800	7. 23. 07	14,65
1875	17 Sep – 25 Sep	CITY OF BERLIN	Inman	”	”	”	2829	7. 18. 02	15,21
1876	27 Oct – 4 Nov	BRITANNIC	White Star	”	”	”	2795	7. 13. 11	15,43
1877	6 Apr – 13 Apr	GERMANIC	”	”	”	”	2830	7. 11. 37	15,76
1882	9 Apr – 16 Apr	ALASKA	Guion Line	”	”	”	2802	7. 06. 20	16,07
1882	14 May – 21 May	ALASKA	”	”	”	”	2871	7. 04. 12	16,67
1882	18 Jun – 25 Jun	ALASKA	”	”	”	”	2886	7. 01. 58	16,98
1883	29 Apr – 6 May	ALASKA	”	”	”	”	2844	6. 23. 48	17,05

Period			Ship's name	Shipping company	Nation	From	To	Nautical miles	Days Hours Min.	knots
1884	13 Apr	– 19 Apr	OREGON	Guion	Britain	Queenstown	Sandy Hook	2861	6. 10. 10	18,56
1885	16 Aug	– 22 Aug	ETRURIA	Cunard	”	”	”	2801	6. 05. 31	18,73
1887	29 May	– 4 Jun	UMBRIA	”	”	”	”	2848	6. 04. 12	19,22
1888	27 May	– 2 Jun	ETRURIA	”	”	”	”	2854	6. 01. 55	19,56
1889	2 May	– 8 May	CITY OF PARIS	Inman & Int.	”	”	”	2855	5. 23. 07	19,95
1889	22 Aug	– 28 Aug	CITY OF PARIS	”	”	”	”	2788	5. 19. 18	20,01
1891	30 Jul	– 5 Aug	MAJESTIC	White Star	”	”	”	2777	5. 18. 08	20,10
1891	13 Aug	– 19 Aug	TEUTONIC	”	”	”	”	2778	5. 16. 31	20,35
1892	20 Jul	– 27 Jul	CITY OF PARIS	Inman & Int.	”	”	”	2785	5. 15. 58	20,48
1892	13 Oct	– 18 Oct	CITY OF PARIS	”	”	”	”	2782	5. 14. 24	20,70
1893	18 Jun	– 23 Jun	CAMPANIA	Cunard	”	”	”	2864	5. 15. 37	21,12
1894	12 Aug	– 17 Aug	CAMPANIA	”	”	”	”	2776	5. 09. 29	21,44
1894	26 Aug	– 31 Aug	LUCANIA	”	”	”	”	2787	5. 08. 38	21,65
1894	23 Sep	– 28 Sep	LUCANIA	”	”	”	”	2782	5. 07. 48	21,75
1894	21 Oct	– 26 Oct	LUCANIA	”	”	”	”	2779	5. 07. 23	21,81
1898	30 Mar	– 5 Apr	KAISER WILHELM DER GROSSE	Nord. Lloyd	Germany	Needles	”	3120	5. 20. 00	22,29
1900	6 Jul	– 12 Jul	DEUTSCHLAND	Hapag	”	Eddystone	”	3044	5. 15. 46	22,42
1900	26 Aug	– 1 Sept	DEUTSCHLAND	”	”	Cherbourg	”	3050	5. 12. 29	23,02
1901	26 Jul	– 1 Aug	DEUTSCHLAND	”	”	”	”	3141	5. 16. 12	23,06
1902	10 Sep	– 16 Sep	KRONPRINZ WILHELM	Nord. Lloyd	”	”	”	3047	5. 11. 57	23,09
1903	2 Sep	– 8 Sep	DEUTSCHLAND	Hapag	”	”	”	3054	5. 11. 54	23,15
1907	6 Oct	– 10 Oct	LUSITANIA	Cunard	Britain	Queenstown	”	2780	4. 19. 52	23,99
1908	17 May	– 21 May	LUSITANIA	”	”	”	”	2889	4. 20. 22	24,83
1908	5 Jul	– 10 Jul	LUSITANIA	”	”	”	”	2891	4. 19. 36	25,01
1909	8 Aug	– 12 Aug	LUSITANIA	”	”	”	Ambrose	2890	4. 16. 40	25,65
1909	26 Sep	– 30 Sep	MAURETANIA	”	”	”	”	2874	4. 10. 51	26,06
1929	17 Jul	– 22 Jul	BREMEN	Nord. Lloyd	Germany	Cherbourg	”	3164	4. 17. 42	27,83
1930	20 Mar	– 25 Mar	EUROPA	”	”	”	”	3157	4. 17. 06	27,91
1933	27 Jun	– 2 Jul	EUROPA	”	”	”	”	3149	4. 16. 48	27,92
1933	11 Aug	– 16 Aug	REX	Italia	Italy	Gibraltar	”	3181	4. 13. 58	28,92
1935	30 May	– 3 Jun	NORMANDIE	C.G. Trans.	France	Bishop Rock	”	2971	4. 03. 02	29,98
1936	20 Aug	– 24 Aug	QUEEN MARY	Cunard	Britain	”	”	2907	4. 00. 27	30,14
1937	29 Jul	– 2 Aug	NORMANDIE	C.G. Trans.	France	”	”	2906	3. 23. 02	30,58
1938	4 Aug	– 8 Aug	QUEEN MARY	Cunard	Britain	”	”	2907	3. 21. 48	30,99
1952	11 Jul	– 15 Jul	UNITED STATES	U.S. Lines	U.S.A.	”	”	2906	3. 12. 12	34,51

†All data in these tables taken from Noel R P Bonsor, *North Atlantic Seaway*, vol 5   °Values for distance and knots calculated subsequently

Record voyages in the eastbound direction, 1838 to 1952

Period		Ship's name	Shipping company	Nation	From	To	Nautical miles	Days Hours Min.	knots
1838	1 May – 19 May	SIRIUS	Brit. & Am.	Britain	New York	Falmouth	3 159	18. 00. 00	07,31°
1838	7 May – 22 May	GREAT WESTERN	Great West.	„	„	Avonmouth	3 218	14. 15. 59	09,14
1838	25 Jun – 8 Jul	GREAT WESTERN	„	„	„	„	3 099	12. 16. 34	10,17
1840	4 Aug – 14 Aug	BRITANNIA	Cunard	„	Halifax	Liverpool	2 610	9. 21. 44	10,98°
1842	28 Apr – 11 May	GREAT WESTERN	Great West.	„	New York	„	3 248	12. 07. 30	10,99
1843	4 Apr – 14 Apr	COLUMBIA	Cunard	„	Halifax	„	2 534	9. 12. 00	11,11°
1843	18 May – 27 May	HIBERNIA	„	„	„	„	2 534	9. 10. 44	11,18°
1843	18 Jul – 27 Jul	HIBERNIA	„	„	„	„	2 534	8. 22. 44	11,80°
1849	19 Jul – 28 Jul	CANADA	„	„	„	„	2 534	8. 12. 44	12,38°
1851	10 May – 20 May	PACIFIC	Collins	U.S.A.	New York	„	3 078	9. 20. 14	13,03
1852	7 Feb – 17 Feb	ARCTIC	„	„	„	„	3 051	9. 17. 15	13,06
1856	2 Apr – 12 Apr	PERSIA	Cunard	Britain	Sandy Hook	„	3 048	9. 10. 22	13,46°
1856	14 May – 23 May	PERSIA	„	„	„	„	3 048	9. 03. 24	13,89°
1856	6 Aug – 15 Aug	PERSIA	„	„	„	„	3 046	8. 23. 19	14,15°
1863	16 Dec – 24 Dec	SCOTIA	„	„	New York	Queenstown	2 800	8. 05. 42	14,16°
1869	4 Dec – 12 Dec	CITY OF BRUSSELS	Inman	„	Sandy Hook	„	2 780	7. 20. 33	14,74°
1873	11 Jan – 19 Jan	BALTIC	White Star	„	„	„	2 840	7. 20. 09	15,09
1875	2 Oct – 10 Oct	CITY OF BERLIN	Inman	„	„	„	2 820	7. 15. 28	15,37
1876	5 Feb – 13 Feb	GERMANIC	White Star	„	„	„	2 894	7. 15. 17	15,79
1876	16 Dec – 24 Dec	BRITANNIC	„	„	„	„	2 882	7. 12. 41	15,94
1879	22 Jul – 29 Jul	ARIZONA	Guion	„	„	„	2 810	7. 08. 11	15,96
1882	30 May – 6 Jun	ALASKA	„	„	„	„	2 791	6. 22. 00	16,81°
1882	12 Sep – 19 Sep	ALASKA	„	„	„	„	2 781	6. 18. 37	17,10
1884	29 Mar – 5 Apr	OREGON	„	„	„	„	2 916	7. 02. 18	17,12
1884	26 Apr – 3 May	OREGON	„	„	„	„	2 911	6. 16. 57	18,09
1884	30 Jul – 7 Aug	OREGON	Cunard	„	„	„	2 853	6. 12. 54	18,18
1884	3 Sep – 10 Sep	OREGON	„	„	„	„	2 853	6. 11. 09	18,39
1885	1 Aug – 7 Aug	ETRURIA	„	„	„	„	2 822	6. 09. 00	18,44
1888	7 Jul – 14 Jul	ETRURIA	„	„	„	„	2 881	6. 04. 50	19,36
1889	15 May – 22 May	CITY OF PARIS	Inman & Int.	„	„	„	2 894	6. 00. 29	20,03
1892	17 Aug – 23 Aug	CITY OF NEW YORK	„	„	„	„	2 814	5. 19. 57	20,11
1893	6 May – 12 May	CAMPANIA	Cunard	„	„	„	2 928	5. 17. 27	21,30
1894	6 May – 12 May	LUCANIA	„	„	„	„	2 911	5. 13. 28	21,81
1894	2 Jun – 8 Jun	LUCANIA	„	„	„	„	2 911	5. 12. 59	21,90
1895	18 May – 24 May	LUCANIA	„	„	„	„	2 897	5. 11. 40	22,00
1897	23 Nov – 29 Nov	KAISER WILHELM DER GROSSE	Nord. Lloyd	Germany	„	Needles	3 065	5. 17. 23	22,33

Period		Ship's name	Shipping company	Nation	From	To	Nautical miles	Days Hours Min.	knots
1900	18 Jul – 24 Jul	DEUTSCHLAND	Hapag	Germany	Sandy Hook	Eddystone	3085	5. 15. 05	22,84
1900	4 Sep – 10 Sep	DEUTSCHLAND	,,	,,	,,	,,	2981	5. 07. 38	23,36
1901	13 Jun – 19 Jun	DEUTSCHLAND	,,	,,	,,	,,	3083	5. 11. 51	23,38
1901	10 Jul – 17 Jul	DEUTSCHLAND	,,	,,	,,	,,	3082	5. 11. 05	23,51
1904	14 Jun – 20 Jun	KAISER WILHELM II	Nord. Lloyd	,,	,,	,,	3112	5. 11. 58	23,58
1907	19 Oct – 24 Oct	LUSITANIA	Cunard	Britain	,,	Queenstown	2807	4. 22. 53	23,61
1907	30 Nov – 5 Dec	MAURETANIA	,,	,,	,,	,,	2807	4. 22. 33	23,69
1908	25 Jan – 30 Jan	MAURETANIA	,,	,,	,,	,,	2932	5. 02. 41	23,90
1908	7 Mar – 12 Mar	MAURETANIA	,,	,,	,,	,,	2932	5. 00. 05	24,42
1909	3 Feb – 8 Feb	MAURETANIA	,,	,,	Ambrose	,,	2930	4. 20. 27	25,16
1909	17 Mar – 22 Mar	MAURETANIA	,,	,,	,,	,,	2934	4. 18. 35	25,61
1909	5 May – 10 May	MAURETANIA	,,	,,	,,	,,	2934	4. 18. 11	25,70
1909	16 Jun – 21 Jun	MAURETANIA	,,	,,	,,	,,	2933	4. 17. 21	25,88
1924	20 Aug – 25 Aug	MAURETANIA	,,	,,	,,	Cherbourg	3198	5. 01. 49	26,25
1929	27 Jul – 1 Aug	BREMEN	Nord. Lloyd	Germany	,,	Eddystone	3084	4. 14. 30	27,91
1933	10 Jun – 15 Jun	BREMEN	,,	,,	,,	Cherbourg	3199	4. 16. 15	28,51
1935	7 Jun – 11 Jun	NORMANDIE	C.G. Trans.	France	,,	Bishop Rock	3015	4. 03. 25	30,31
1936	26 Aug – 30 Aug	QUEEN MARY	Cunard-W.S.	Britain	,,	,,	2939	3. 23. 57	30,63
1937	18 Mar – 22 Mar	NORMANDIE	C.G. Trans.	France	,,	,,	2967	4. 00. 06	30,99
1937	4 Aug – 8 Aug	NORMANDIE	,,	,,	,,	,,	2936	3. 22. 07	31,20
1938	10 Aug – 14 Aug	QUEEN MARY	Cunard-W.S.	Britain	,,	,,	2938	3. 20. 42	31,69
1952	3 Jul – 7 Jul	UNITED STATES	U.S. Lines	U.S.A.	,,	,,	2942	3. 10. 40	35,59

°Values for distance and knots calculated subsequently

Record for the 'Blue Riband, 2nd class', eastbound

Period	Record ship in eastbound direction	Holder of the Blue Riband
Aug 1840 – Jun 1841	BRITANNIA	GREAT WESTERN
Apr 1842 – Apr 1843	GREAT WESTERN	COLUMBIA
Apr 1843 – May 1843	COLUMBIA	GREAT WESTERN
May 1843 – Jul 1843	HIBERNIA	GREAT WESTERN
Jul 1845 – Jun 1848	HIBERNIA	CAMBRIA
Jun 1848 – Oct 1848	HIBERNIA	AMERICA
Oct 1848 – Jul 1849	CANADA	EUROPA
May 1850 – Sep 1850	CANADA	ASIA
Sep 1850 – May 1851	CANADA	PACIFIC
May 1851 – Aug 1851	PACIFIC	BALTIC
Feb 1852 – Apr 1856	ARCTIC	BALTIC
Dec 1869 – May 1872	CITY OF BRUSSELS	SCOTIA
May 1872 – Jan 1873	CITY OF BRUSSELS	ADRIATIC
Jan 1873 – Jul 1875	BALTIC	ADRIATIC
Jul 1875 – Sep 1875	BALTIC	GERMANIC
Sep 1875 – Okt 1875	BALTIC	CITY OF BERLIN
Oct 1875 – Feb 1876	CITY OF BERLIN	BRITANNIC
Feb 1876 – Oct 1876	GERMANIC	BRITANNIC
Dec 1876 – Apr 1877	BRITANNIC	GERMANIC
Jul 1879 – Apr 1882	ARIZONA	GERMANIC
May 1887 – May 1888	ETRURIA	UMBRIA
Jul 1891 – Aug 1891	CITY OF PARIS	MAJESTIC
Aug 1891 – Jul 1892	CITY OF PARIS	TEUTONIC
Aug 1892 – Jun 1893	CITY OF NEW YORK	CITY OF PARIS
Jun 1894 – Aug 1894	LUCANIA	CAMPANIA
Nov 1897 – Mar 1898	KAISER WILHELM DER GROSSE	LUCANIA
Sep 1902 – Sep 1903	DEUTSCHLAND	KRONPRINZ WILHELM
Jun 1904 – Oct 1907	KAISER WILHELM II	DEUTSCHLAND
Oct 1907 – Jun 1909	MAURETANIA	LUSITANIA
Mar 1930 – Aug 1933	BREMEN	EUROPA
Aug 1933 – Jun 1935	BREMEN	REX

The table printed here lists those ships whose eastbound records were not held by the holder of the Blue Riband at that time, – ie it covers only those periods when it was possible to speak of two ships simultaneously 'holding the Blue Riband'.

The list also states the duration of the 'divided title' situation, together with the name of the ship which actually held the Blue Riband in the same period, by dint of a record crossing in the westerley direction.

The ships whose names are underlined held the eastbound record only, whereas all the others held the Blue Riband at different times in addition to the eastbound record.

Detailed specification of all holders of the Blue Riband

The table on the following two pages has been assembled on the basis of careful analysis of all the literature sources mentioned; the information is that which was valid at the time the ships were commissioned. I have attempted to explain contradictions by cross-referencing and by critical assessment of the source material. In the case of the older ships (pre-1870) I have stated the engine power as the highest and lowest of the nominal values, but I cannot be absolutely certain that these figures actually represent the normal sustainable power and the maximum possible power. It has proved impossible to determine some of the individual data; in such cases the entry has been left vacant. In contrast, a hyphen in the table indicates that the data does not apply.

Key to the table entries:

1 Construction material: H = wood, E = iron, all others steel.

4 Dipl is the water displacement of the fully equipped ship. In the case of British ships the unit is the Imperial ton of 2240lbs; in the case of German ships the metric tonne of 1000kg.

5 LOA is the overall length in feet, but excluding any bowsprit or similar item;
   Reg is the registered length in feet, usually as shown in Lloyd's Register.

6 Beam is the maximum breadth of the hull in feet to the outside of the frames, generally called the moulded breadth.

7 L:B is the registered length to beam in feet; Tg – draught in feet.

8 D = number of full-length decks.
   S = number of watertight bulkheads.

10 HD, MD, ND – high-pressure, intermediate-pressure and low-pressure. Hub = Piston Stroke. Rpm = Revolutions per minute of the screw at service speed.

11 KK = trunk boiler, FK = fire tube boiler, ZK = cylindrical boiler, WK = water tube boiler; at = atmospheric vapour pressure.

12 Heating area in square metres; number of furnaces.

13 Engine power in indicated HP (ihp), and shaft HP (shp) respectively; top figure contract power, bottom figure maximum power. For comparative purposes: ihp:shp is approximately 5:4.

14 S = number of screw propellers; F = number of propeller blades per shaft; Ø = diameter of propeller or of paddle wheel in feet.

15 Knots = nautical miles at 6080ft per hour. Top figure sustainable service speed, bottom figure maximum continuous performance when winning the Blue Riband.

16 Top figure = daily fuel consumption in tons/tonnes; bottom figure – bunker capacity in tons or tonnes.

17 I., II., III. = number of passengers in the three classes. On *Bremen*, *Europa* and *Rex* the total of the two middle classes is included under II.; in the case of III the steerage facilities are included. Crew = number of crew.

1 Name / Building material / Shipping company	2 Launch / Delivery	3 Shipyard, Place; Yard. No.	4 grt / Displ.	5 LOA / Reg. length	6 Beam / Depth	7 L:B / Tg	8 D / S	9 Engine type / Manufacturer	10 HD ND	10 MD Hub	10 ND°° rpm	11 Boiler / at	12 Heating area / furnaces	13 PSi norm. / PSi max.	14 S F / Ø	15 Knots / max	16 Fuel / Bunk	17 I. II. / III. Crew
SIRIUS (H) / Brit. & Amer., Liverp.	1837 / 1837	Robert Menzies & Son, Leith	703 / 1995	200 / 178	25 / 20	23	2	1 2-cyl.-side lever / Wingate	– / –			2 KK / 1.0	/ 8	600	Paddle / 26.3	7.50	24 / –	– / 37
GREAT WESTERN (H) / Great Western, Liverp.	19.07.1837 / 31.03.1838	Will. Patterson, Bristol	1340 / 2300	235 / 212	35.3 / 25	19.7 / 16.7	2	1 2-cyl.-side lever / Maudsley	– / –	– / 2133	2x 1855 / 16	4 KK / 1.0	356 / 12	750	Paddle / 32.9	8.50 / 8.53	30 / 600	128 20 / – 60
COLUMBIA (H) / Cunard Line, Liverpool	9.1840 / 1840	Robert Steele & Son, Greenock	1175 / 2050	230 / 207	34 / 22.5	20	2	1 2-cyl.-side lever / Napier	– / –	– / 1854	2x 1841 / 16	4 KK / 0.7	/ 12	740	Paddle / 28.4	9.00 / 9.78	37 / 640	115 / –
CAMBRIA (H) / Cunard Line, Liverpool	1.08.1844 / 1844	Robert Steele & Son, Greenock	1423	240 / 219	37	19.4	2	1 2-cyl.-side lever / Napier	– / –			4 KK / 0.7		1040	Paddle / 28.4	9.00	/ 740	120 / – 90
AMERICA (H) / Cunard Line, Liverpool	13.05.1847 / 4.1848	Robert Steele & Son, Greenock	1825	270 / 251	38 / 25.3	21.7	2	1 2-cyl.-side lever / Napier	–	– / 2438	2x 2254 / 16	4 KK / 0.9	/ 16	1400	Paddle / 38.4	10.00	60 / 840	140 / –
EUROPA (H) / Cunard Line, Liverpool	22.09.1847 / 7.1848	John Wood, Port Glasgow	1834	270 / 251	38 / 25.3	21.7	2	1 2-cyl.-side lever / Napier	–	– / 2438	2x 2254 / 16	4 KK / 0.9	/ 16	1400	Paddle / 38.4	10.00	60 / 840	140 / –
ASIA (H) / Cunard Line, Liverpool	31.01.1850 / 5.1850	Robert Steele & Son, Greenock	2227 / 3620	290 / 266	40 / 24	22 / 19	2	1 2-cyl.-side lever / Napier	–	– / 3048	2x 2438	4 KK / 0.9	/ 24	2000 / 2150	Paddle / 37.7	12.00 / 12.25	76 / 809	130 30 / 112
PACIFIC (H) / Collins Line, New York	1.02.1849 / 5.1850	Jacob Bell, New York	2707 / 6000	295 / 281	45 / 31.5	20.7	2	1 2-cyl.-side lever / Allaire	–	– / 3047	2x 2438	4 KK / 1.2	/ 32	2000 / 2500	Paddle / 40.9	12.00	85	200 / – 145
BALTIC (H) / Collins Line, New York	5.02.1850 / 11.1850	Jacob Bell, New York	2723 / 6000	296.5 / 282	45 / 31.5	20.7	2	1 2-cyl.-side lever / Allaire	–	– / 3047	2x 2438	4 KK / 1.2	/ 32	2000 / 2500	Paddle / 42.8	12.00	85	200 / – 145
PERSIA (E) / Cunard Line, Liverpool	3.07.1855 / 8.01.1856	Robert Napier & Sons, Glasgow	3300 / 8600	398 / 375	45 / 30	26.2 / 23.6	2 / 6	1 2-cyl.-side lever / Napier	–	– / 2540	2x 2539 / 17	8 KK / 1.4	/ 40	3600 / 4750	Paddle / 40	13.00 / 13.11	145 / 1600	200 / 50
SCOTIA (E) / Cunard Line, Liverpool	25.06.1861 / 3.1862	Robert Napier & Sons, Glasgow	3871 / 8755	400 / 382	47.8 / 30.4	26.2	2 / 6	1 2-cyl.-side lever / Napier	3048	–	2539	8 KK / 1.2	2556 / 40	4000 / 4900	Paddle / 40	13.50 / 14.46	164 / 1800	273 / 50
ADRIATIC (E) / White Star, Liverpool	17.10.1871 / 31.03.1872	Harland & Wolff, Belfast; 77	3868 / 7450	454 / 437	40.8 / 31	35 / 23.6	2	1 4-cyl. Compound / Maudslay	–	2x 1041 / 1524	2x 1981	10 FK / 4.6	/ 20	3000 / 3200	1 4 / 23.4	14.00 / 14.53	65 / –	166 / – 1000
GERMANIC (E) / White Star, Liverpool	15.07.1874 / 24.04.1875	Harland & Wolff, Belfast; 85	5008 / 9600	468 / 455	45 / 33.7	32.8	2 / 7	1 4-cyl. Compound / Maudslay	–	2x 1117 / 1524	2x 2108	8 FK / 5.3	1806 / 32	5000 / 5500	/ 51.7	15.00	110 / 1100	220 1500 / – 130
CITY OF BERLIN (E) / Inman Line, Liverpool	27.10.1874 / 4.1875	Caird & Co., Greenock	5491 / 10100	520 / 488	44 / 35	37.7	2	1 dbl. Compound / Caird	–	1829 / 1651	3048 / 62	12 FK / 5.3	1463 / 36	4800 / 5200	1 5 / 21.5	15.00 / 15.21	120 / 1400	170 100 / 1500
BRITANNIC (E) / White Star, Liverpool	3.02.1874 / 6.06.1874	Harland & Wolff, Belfast; 83	5004 / 9600	468 / 455	45 / 33.7	33.1 / 23.6	2 / 7	1 4-cyl. Compound* / Maudslay	–	2x 1219 / 1524	2x 2108	8 FK / 5.3	/ 32	5000 / 5500		15.00 / 15.43	110 / 1100	220 1500 / – 135
ALASKA (E) / Guion Line, Liverpool	15.07.1881 / 10.1881	John Elder & Co, Glasgow; 247	6932 / 9210	520 / 500	50 / 38	32.8	4 / 9	1 3-cyl. Compound / Elder	– / 1828	1727	2x 2539	9 FK / 7.0	/ 54	8300 / 11000	1 4 / 23	16.00 / 17.05	250 / –	350 / – 1000
OREGON (E) / Guion Line, Liverpool	23.06.1883 / 9.1883	John Elder & Co, Glasgow	7375 / 12500	520 / 501	54 / 40	30.2 / 24.9	4 / 9	1 3-cyl. Compound / Elder	–	1777 / 1829	2x 2640 / 64	9 FK / 7.7	3523 / 72	12500 / 13500		17.50 / 18.56	268 / 2360	340 92 / 1110 255
ETRURIA (E) / Cunard Line, Liverpool	20.09.1884 / 4.1885	John Elder & Co, Glasgow; 286	7718 / 13300	519 / 501.5	57 / 38	28.9	4 / 9	1 3-cyl. Compound / Elder	–	1803 / 1828	2x 2666 / 68	9 FK / 7.7	4212 / 72	14500	1 4	19.00 / 19.56	315	550 160 / 800
UMBRIA (E) / Cunard Line. Liverpool	26.06.1884 / 10.1884	John Elder & Co, Glasgow; 258	7718 / 13300	519 / 501.5	57 / 38	28.9	4 / 9	1 3-cyl. Compound / Elder	–	1803 / 1828	2x 2666 / 68	9 FK / 7.7	4212 / 72	14500	1 4	19.00 / 19.22	315	550 160 / 800

1 Name Shipping company / Building material	2 Launch Delivery	3 Shipyard, Place; Yard No.	4 grt Displ.	5 LOA Reg. length	6 Beam Depth	7 L:B Tg	8 D S	9 Engine type Manufacturer	10 HD ND	MD Hub	ND°° rpm	11 Boiler at	12 Heating area furnaces	13 PSi norm. PSi max.	14 S F Ø	15 Knots max	16 Fuel Bunk	17 I. II. / III. Crew
CITY OF PARIS / Inman & Inter., Liverp.	23.10.1888 / 3.1889	J.& G. Thomson, Glasgow	10499 / 17270	560 / 527.5	63 / 39.2	29.2 / 26.6	4 / 14	2 tri. exp. / Thomson	1143 / 1524	1803	2869 / 89	9 FK / 10.5	4654 / 54	18000 / 18500	2 3 / 19.5	20.00 / 20.70	300	540 / 200 / 1000 / 362
MAJESTIC / White Star, Liverpool	29.06.1889 / 23.03.1890	Harland & Wolff, Belfast; 209	9965 / 16740	582 / 567.7	57.8 / 39	32.5 / 24	3 / 13	2 tri. exp. / Harl. & W.	1092 / 1524	1727	2793	12 FK / 12.6	3710 / 76	17500 / 19500	2 3 / 19.5	20.00 / 20.10	320	300 / 190 / 1000
TEUTONIC / White Star, Liverpool	19.01.1889 / 25.07.1890	Harland & Wolff, Belfast; 208	9984 / 16740	582 / 567.7	57.8 / 39	32.5 / 24	3 / 13	2 tri. exp. / Harl. & W.	1092 / 1524	1727	2793	12 FK / 12.6	3710 / 76	17500 / 19500	2 3 / 19.5	20.00 / 20.35	320	300 / 190 / 1000
CAMPANIA / Cunard Line, Liverpool	8.09.1892 / 14.03.1893	Fairfield Co., Glasgow; 364	12950 / 18450	622 / 600.9	65 / 41.6	30.5 / 29.9	4 / 16	2 5-cyl. tri. exp. / Fairfield	2x1447 / –	2006 / 1752	2x2489 / 82	12 FK / 11.6	7821 / 96	30000 / 30150	28	21.00 / 21.44	485 / 3160	600 / 400 / 1000 / 415
LUCANIA / Cunard Line, Liverpool	2.02.1893 / 8.1893	Fairfield Co., Glasgow; 365	12952 / 18000	622 / 600.9	65 / 41.6	30.5 / 29.9	4 / 16	2 5-cyl. tri. exp. / Fairfield	2x1447 / –	2006 / 1752	2x2489 / 82	12 FK / 11.6	7821 / 96	30000 / 30150	28	21.00 / 21.44	485 / 3160	600 / 400 / 1000 / 415
KAISER WILH. D. GROSSE / Nordd. Lloyd, Bremen	4.05.1897 / 12.09.1897	AG Vulcan, Stettin; 234	14349 / 20880	648.5 / 626.7	66 / 39	31.2 / 27.9	4 / 16	2 4-cyl. tri. exp. / Vulcan	1320 / –	2x2279 / 1752	2450 / 75	14 ZK / 12.5	7830 / 104	27000 / 31000	2 4 / 21.4	22.00 / 22.29	4500	206 / 226 / 1074 / 488
DEUTSCHLAND / Hamburg-Amerika, Hbg	10.01.1900 / 25.06.1900	AG Vulcan, Stettin; 244	16502 / 23600	684 / 660.9	67.2 / 40.3	32.2 / 28.9	4 / 16	2 quad. exp.° / Vulcan	930 / 2850	1885 / 1850	2639 / 76	16 ZK / 15.0	7940 / 112	34000 / 37800	2 4 / 22.3	22.50 / 23.15	500 / 4850	429 / 226 / 284 / 557
KRONPRINZ WILHELM / Nordd. Lloyd, Bremen	30.03.1901 / 29.08.1901	AG Vulcan, Stettin; 249	14908 / 21300	663.3 / 637.3	66.2 / 39.3	31.5 / 28.9	4 / 18	2 6-cyl. quad. exp.° / Vulcan	2x865 / 2x2590	1752 / 2006	2490	16 ZK / 15.0	8720 / 112	33000 / 36000	2 4 / 21.4	22.50 / 23.09	500 / 4500	301 / 300 / 717 / 528

Name Shipping company / Building material	Launch Delivery	Shipyard, Place; Yard No.	grt Displ.	LOA Reg. length	Beam Depth	L:B Tg	D S	Engine type Manufacturer	rpm	Boiler at	Heating area furnaces	PSW norm. PSW max.	S F Ø	Knots max	Fuel Bunk	I. II. / III. Crew
LUSITANIA / Cunard Line, Liverpool	7.06.1906 / 26.08.1907	John Brown & Co, Glasgow; 802	31550 / 38000	786 / 762	88 / 44	29.5 / 33.5	4 / 15	2 high-pressure, 2 low-pressure turbines, / Brown	180	25 ZK / 13.7	14662 / 192	68000 / 76000	4 3	25.00 / 25.65	850 / 6030	563 / 464 / 1138 / 802
MAURETANIA / Cunard Line, Liverpool	20.09.1906 / 7.11.1907	S., H. & W. R., Wallsend; 735	31938 / 38000	790 / 762	88 / 15.2	29.5 / 33.5	4 / 15	2 high-pressure, 2 low-pressure turbines, / Wallsend	180	25 ZK / 13.7	14722 / 192	68000 / 78260	4 3	25.00 / 25.65	850 / 6350	563 / 464 / 1138 / 802
BREMEN / Nordd. Lloyd, Bremen	16.08.1928 / 5.07.1929	Deschimag, Bremen; 872	51656 / 55600	938.6 / 898.6	101.7 / 48.2	27.6 / 32.2	6 / 14	4 sets geared turbines, / Deschimag	180	20 WK / 23.0	17050 / 227	105000 / 130000	4 4 / 16.4	26.30 / 27.83	850 / 7552	811 / 800 / 617 / 966
EUROPA / Nordd. Lloyd, Bremen	15.08.1928 / 17.03.1930	Blohm & Voss, Hamburg; 479	49746 / 56390	936.7 / 890.2	101.7 / 48	27.6 / 32.2	6 / 14	4 sets geared turbines, / Blohm & Voss	180	24 WK / 22.0	16800 / 240	105000 / 136400	4 4 / 16.4	26.30 / 27.92	800 / 6676	860 / 805 / 600 / 965
REX / Italia, Genua	1.08.1931 / 9.1932	Ansaldo, Genua; 296	51062 / 45800	880 / 833.8	97 / 46	28.2 / 32.2	5 / 14	4 sets geared turbines, / Ansaldo	230	12 WK / 26.5	18000 / 216	100000 / 142000	4 4	27.50 / 28.92	900 / 9700	408 / 768 / 866 / 756
NORMANDIE / C.G. Transat., Le Havre	29.10.1932 / 5.05.1935	Penhoët, St. Nazaire; T6	79280 / 67500	1,029 / 981.4	118 / 54	27.2 / 36.4	7 / 11	4 each turbines, generators, and electric motors, Alsthom	180	29 WK / 28.0	29000 / 225	130000 / 165000	4 3 / 16	28.50 / 30.58	6400	848 / 670 / 454 / 1345
QUEEN MARY / Cunard Line, Liverpool	26.09.1934 / 15.04.1936	John Brown, Glasgow; 534	80774 / 67200	1,019.4 / 975	118.5 / 68.5	26.9 / 38.7	5 / 19	4 sets geared turbines, / Brown		24 WK / 28.7	158000 / 168	200000	4 4 / 20	29.00 / 30.99	1020 / 6830	776 / 784 / 579 / 1101
UNITED STATES / U.S. Lines, New York	23.06.1951 / 21.06.1952	Newport News, Newp.News; 488	53329 / 56000	990 / 907.7	101.6	29.5 / 32.2	4	4 sets geared turbines, / Westinghouse		8 WK / 68.6		173000 / 242000	4 4+	31.00 / 40.00	12080	871 / 508 / 549 / 1093

° Tandem construction, high-pressure cylinder arranged above low-pressure cylinder.

°° On quadruple-expansion engines this is an intermediate-pressure (MP) cylinder.

+ Two 4-bladed, two 5-bladed propellers.

Bibliography

Anderson, Roy, *White Star* (Prescot 1964)

Barbance, Marthe, *Histoire de la Compagnie Générale Transatlantique* (Paris 1955)

Benstead, C R, *Atlantic Ferry* (London 1936)

Bertram, Georg, *Aus der Zeit der großen Schnelldampfer* (Bremen 1997)

Bonsor, Noel R P, *North Atlantic Seaway*, vols 1–5 (Newton Abbot and Brookside 1975 to 1980)

'The Blue Riband of the North Atlantic', *The Shipbuilder and Marine Engine Builder* 1936, pp528–532

Braynard, Frank O, *S.S. Savannah* (Athens 1963)

Eliseo, Maurizio, *Rex* (Parma 1992)

Fry, Henry, *The History of North Atlantic Steam Navigation* (London 1896)

Hales, H K, *The Autobiography of 'The Card'* (London 1937)

Haws, Duncan, *Merchant Fleets in Profile*, vol 2 (Cambridge 1979) and vol 12 (Burwash 1987)

Hughes, Tom, *Der Kampf ums Blaue Band* (Oldenburg and Hamburg 1974)

Isherwood, John H, 'Steamers of the Past' *Sea Breezes*. *Adratic* vol 23, 1957/*Alaska*, vol 10, 1950/*Arizona*, vol 24, 1957/*Campania* and

Lucania, vol 16, 1953/*City of Berlin*, vol 18, 1954/*City of New York*, vol 31, 1961/*City of Paris*, vol 8, 1949/*Germanic*, vol 19, 1955/*Kaiser Wilhelm der Grosse*, vol 10, 1950/*Kaiser Wilhelm II*, vol 59, 1986/*Lusitania*, vol 34, 1962/*Majestic*, vol 41, 1967/*Mauretania*, vol 45, 1971/*Persia*, vol 40, 1966/*Rex*, vol 53, 1979/*Scotia*, vol 11, 1951

Kludas, Arnold, Die deutschen Schnelldampfer, *Deutsches Schiffahrtsarchiv* (DSA) vol I 'Die Flüsse-Klasse des North Germann Lloyds', DSA 3.1980; vol II, 'Die *Augusta-Victoria-Klasse*', DSA 4.1981; vol III, 'Vierschornsteiner', DSA 6.1983; vol IV, 'Die *Imperator*-Klasse', DSA 8.1985; vol V, '*Bremen* and *Europa*', DSA 11.1988.

Kludas, Arnold, *Die Geschichte der deutschen Passagierschiffahrt*, vols 1–5 (Hamburg 1986–1990)

Kludas, Arnold, *Die großen Passagierschiffe der Welt*, vols 1–5 (Oldenburg und Hamburg 1972–1974)

Kludas, Arnold, *Die Schnelldampfer Bremen* and *Europa* (Herford 1993)

Lee, Charles E, *The Blue Riband* (London 1931)

Mackenzie-Kennedy, Chess, *The Atlantic Blue Riband* (York 1993)

Maginnis, Arthur J, *The Atlantic Ferry* (London 1892)

O'Sullivan, Patrick, *The Lusitania* (Cork 1998)

Potter, Neil and Jack Frost, *The Queen Mary* (New York 1961)

'Transatlantic Challenge 1990', *Lloyd's List International* (London 1990)

Trogoff, Jean, *La course au Ruban Bleu* (Paris 1945)

Winchester, Clarence, *Shipping Wonders of the World*, vols I and II. (London 1935/36)

Williams, David L and Richard P de Kerbrech, *Damned by Destiny* (Brighton 1982)

The following journals were consulted, particularly for technical details.

Engineering

Lloyd's Register of Shipping

Schiffbau

Shipbuilding and Shipping Record

The Shipbuilder

Zeitschrift des Vereins deutscher Ingenieure

Werft – Reederei – Hafen

Picture references

Blohm + Voss GmbH, Hamburg:
110.

Dietmar Borchert, Bergen-Eversen:
35, 39, 40, 45, 47, 48, 53, 54, 57, 62, 68, 72, 77, 79, 84, 85, 93, 97, 104, 105, 115, 119, 126, 130, 135, 142.

Frank O. Braynard, Sea Cliff:
35 r., 125 r.

Deutsches Schiffahrtsmuseum, Bremerhaven:
58, 62 o, 69, 73.

Christian Eckhardt, Bexhövede:
18

Maurizio Eliseo, Genoa:
118 l., 119, 120, 121, 144.

Hapag-Lloyd AG, Hamburg:
2, 76.

Wilhelm Kluth, Bremerhaven:
137.

Foto Flite Skyfotos, Ashford:
140.

J F Horst Koenig, Hamburg:
28, 29.

Staatsarchiv Hamburg:
96.

Ulster Folk and Transport Museum, Department of Archival Collections:
21, 24.

University of Liverpool Library:
25 (top)

Illustrations were taken from the following books.

Roy Anderson, *White Star*:
55.

Marthe Barbance, *Histoire de la Compagnie Générale Transatlantique*:
122.

Arthur J Maginnis, *The Atlantic Ferry*:
31, 43 r, 44 l, 52, 55 r, 56 l, 57 r, 59 r, 71.

Morskoi Flot:
34.

Winchester, *Shipping Wonders of the World*:
131.

All other illustrations are taken from the author's archive, and consist of photographs, postcards, archive pictures and historic shipping company brochures.

Index